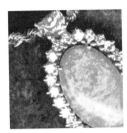

JEWELRY IN THE BIBLE:

What You Always Wanted to Know but
Were Afraid to Ask

ANGEL MANUEL RODRÌGUEZ

Biblical Research Institute
General Conference
Silver Spring, MD

Published by

Ministerial Association
General Conference of Seventh-day Adventists
12501 Old Columbia Pike
Silver Spring, Maryland 20904-6600

Copyright © 1999
PRINTED IN U.S.A.
Pacific Press Publishing Association
1350 North Kings Road
Nampa, Idaho 83687

The author assumes responsibility for the accuracy of all facts and quotations cited in this book.

ISBN 1-57847-054-4

TO THE READER

Controversy continues to grow around whether jewelry can or should have a place in the committed Christian life. This small book is designed to help the reader cut a path through the maze of questions, opinions, and even passions to arrive at genuinely biblical answers. It responds to requests made to the Biblical Research Institute from church leaders, pastors, and interested lay people for a review of the subject. Dr Angel Manuel Rodríguez, associate director of the Institute, was requested to do a serious study of how the Bible deals with jewelry and how the Seventh-day Adventist understanding compares.

The chapters you find here were reviewed by the Biblical Research Institute Committee, a group of more than 30 Bible scholars and teachers. In the process of sometimes spirited discussions, but always marked by Christian dignity, numerous suggestions emerged that have strengthened the final product.

Because of its special value for pastors, elders, and interested lay people, the Ministerial Association of the General Conference joins with the Biblical Research Institute in producing and making available copies of this book. Dr Rodríguez has shared major sections of his findings with pastors in several ministerial councils, where the insights received vigorous positive reception. We believe this book will make a lasting contribution to Christian growth in believers who want the Bible to speak to them despite the confusion of contemporary values drawn from every direction. We are grateful to Dr Rodríguez for his many days spent probing the Scriptures and writing, as well as to the members of the Biblical Research Committee and other reviewers whose helpful suggestions add to the value of the book.

George W Reid, Director
Biblical Research Institute

James A Cress, Executive Secretary
Ministerial Association

CONTENTS

INTRODUCTION

I

It is often said that the subject of jewelry is one on which we should not spend much time. This is true in many ways. There are other much more important subjects that deserve our attention. However, when dealing with this subject we are exploring the nature of the Christian life, the function of biblical principles and standards, and their relationship to justification by faith in Christ. Yes, jewelry is a detail, perhaps a small detail, but it opens a larger field of study because it confronts us not just with our Savior but also with a Lord who makes full claim on every aspect of our lives.

A. Purpose and Definition

This study is fundamentally a Bible study on the function of jewelry in the Bible and its implications for our church members around the world. We will make a special effort to allow the biblical text to speak for itself. Biases? Yes; I write as a Seventh-day Adventist who accepts the Church's standard on ornamental jewelry. But my main interest is to examine all the relevant biblical materials in order to determine whether the standard is biblical or not, or whether it needs adjustment.

Since I will be constantly using the term "jewelry" it is important for the reader to know what I mean by it. "Jewelry" is used in this document to refer to *ornaments made of different materials, with different functions, that can be placed directly on the body or on the garments of a person in order to enhance the appearance of the individual, establish social distinctions, and communicate personal convictions*. This definition is based on my analysis of the biblical materials on this subject.

B. Organization of the Discussion

At times our exposition of this topic may sound too technical and perhaps difficult to follow, but summaries at the end of almost every primary section will facilitate comprehension of the materials. The reader will find significant number of footnotes whose purpose is to cite reference works for those interested in further study, to develop ideas that cannot be placed in the main text, and to evaluate more technical arguments. The nature of the topic requires this type of approach.

We begin by looking at recent trends in the Adventist church respecting attitudes toward the traditional standard on jewelry. We will identify some of the forces that have led to the present debate and issues that need to be addressed. Most of the research concentrates on an analysis of the biblical materials in order to understand their perspective on the subject of jewelry. At the end we will explore implications for the church and its members. But before we begin our study we need briefly to clarify the foundation of all Christian standards.

C. Foundation of Christian Standards

I must state from the very beginning that the acceptance of the Adventist standard on jewelry makes no particular contribution to our salvation and should not occupy the center of our lives. Christianity is centered on the person and work of Christ on behalf of the human family and nothing else should be allowed to occupy that coveted and privileged position. Christ's sacrificial death is the only and exclusive way of access to God and only through him are we accepted by our heavenly Father. According to the Scriptures, this is all a gift of divine grace in which human accomplishments play no meritorious role at all. Every doctrine or standard of the Church must contribute to the unfolding of the meaning of the cross, pointing to its implications for the Christian life.

A Christian lifestyle is determined primarily by God's redemptive work in Christ, being the loving response of a grateful heart to God's unmerited manifestation of love towards a rebellious race.[1] Fallen human beings belong to God through creation, but they are also His property through redemption. Redemption is not only restoration to fellowship with God through His Son, but it also seeks to restore in us the original image of God. The saving efficacy of the death of Christ has a transforming power of such a magnitude that it can, through the work of the Spirit, recreate every human being into the likeness of the Savior.

God has not left it to us to find out or determine how this glorious transformation is to take place. He has spoken to us through the Scriptures and through His Son, through the Word and through a magnificent Model, concerning the nature of the Christian life. Moreover, He has provided for us the guidance and power of the Spirit to enable us to actually become what He intends us to be. It is in submission to God's loving care for us that we are to grow into the likeness of our Savior and Lord.

Therefore, it should not surprise us to find much emphasis in the Scriptures on how believers should relate to God, to other believers, to

[1]Standards for the Christian life are not incompatible with justification by faith; see J. Robert Spangler, "Righteousness by Faith and Standards," *Ministry*, October 1989, pp. 30,31.

society at large, and even to the remainder of the created world. Our fallness has darkened our perceptions of right and wrong, making it necessary for God to instruct us concerning His will. It is by listening to Him and by following Him that we find meaning and self-worth for our lives. To a significant extent the Bible is a description of the kind of life that those who found in Christ their Savior are to enjoy fully, now and throughout eternity. Biblical principles and standards for the Christian life are in fact extremely important because they are God's instruments, through the work of the Spirit, in the internalization of heavenly values and in the concrete expression of a celestial lifestyle on this planet.

Adventists are interested in the proclamation of the gospel and in calling humans to a humble submission to the will of God as revealed in the Bible. Consequently, they have not only underlined the importance of obedience to the Law of God but also the value of a series of specific biblical standards dealing with our spirituality, health and temperance, social life, stewardship, and the simplicity of the Christian life. The Lordship of Christ encompasses every dimension of the human being and by doing that it transforms and enriches our lives. In this study, as indicated above, we will explore one of those aspects, namely the use of jewelry.

Recent Trends in the Adventist Standard on Jewelry

II

A. Position of the Church on Personal Adornment

Among the Fundamental Beliefs of Seventh-day Adventists, belief number 21 summarizes the position of the Church on the standard of personal adornment: "While recognizing cultural differences, our dress is to be simple, modest, and neat, befitting those whose true beauty does not consist of outward adornment but in the imperishable ornament of a gentle and quiet spirit."[1] This is expanded a little more in the *Church Manual*, in the chapter entitled "Standards of Christian Living," as follows: "It is clearly taught in the Scriptures that the wearing of jewelry is contrary to the will of God. '. . . not with braided hair, or gold, or costly array' is the admonition of the apostle Paul (1 Tim. 2:9). The wearing of ornaments of jewelry is a bid for attention which is not in keeping with Christian self-forgetfulness."[2] A quotation from E. G. White is included in that same paragraph, which states that, "To dress plainly, abstaining from display of jewelry and ornaments of every kind, is in keeping with our faith."[3]

However, the *Manual* introduces what seems to be an exception to the standard by allowing the use of wedding rings in countries where it is considered to be "a criterion of virtue, and hence it is not regarded

---

[1] *Seventh-day Adventist Church Manual* (Hagerstown, MD: Review and Herald, 1995), p. 14. The original draft of Fundamental Belief # 21 submitted to the 1980 General Conference Session in Dallas, Texas, included an explicit reference to jewelry. It stated: "We are to dress neatly and modestly, avoiding ostentation and jewelry while seeking instead the ornament of a meek and quiet spirit" ("Fundamental Beliefs of Seventh-day Adventists," *Adventist Review*, February 21, 1980). During the discussion of Belief #21, the delegates made different comments and suggestions but no explicit comment was made concerning the reference to jewelry. Apparently there was nothing objectionable to it. The consensus was that Belief # 21 should be rewritten and expressed in a positive literary style ("Eleventh Business Session," *Adventist Review*, April 25, 1980, pp.20, 31). This was done and as a result the reference to jewelry was deleted from the document. Perhaps the drafters thought the statement should express basic principles rather than specific details. The details were to be stated in the *Church Manual*.

[2] Ibid., p. 150.

[3] E. G. White, *Testimonies to the Church*, vol. 3 (Nampa, ID Pacific Press, 1948), p. 366.

as an ornament."[1] In this the *Manual* is simply echoing the position taken by E. G. White on this subject. Writing to missionaries she said,

> Some have had a burden in regard to the wearing of a marriage ring, feeling that the wives of our ministers should conform to this custom. All this is unnecessary. . . . Americans can make their position understood by plainly stating that the custom is not regarded as obligatory in our country. . . . In countries where the custom is imperative, we have no burden to condemn those who have their marriage ring; let them wear it if they can do so conscientiously; but let not our missionaries feel that the wearing of the ring will increase their influence one jot or tittle.[2]

It is obvious that the Adventist position on the use of jewelry for personal ornamentation is based on certain biblical passages and the support given to it by E. G. White. The principle underlying the standard is identified as self-denial manifested in humble submission to the will of God. The apparent exception is not understood to be, technically speaking, a true exception, for the wedding ring is not considered to be an ornament but a "criterion of virtue." In general that has been the teaching and practice of the Church around the world, but it has never been easy to fully enforce the standard on jewelry.[3] In the last part of the 20th century, some church members, and in some cases church workers in North America, have questioned the traditional Adventist understanding of the wedding band. This new attitude seems to have been influenced by trends in society during and after the Second World War.

B. Wedding Ring Controversy

During the Second World War North America began to experience a change of attitude toward the wedding ring. Its use became popular and important as young brides were separated from their husbands who went

---

[1] *Church Manual*, p. 150.

[2] E. G. White, *Testimonies to Ministers and Gospel Workers* (Nampa, ID: Pacific Press, 1962), pp. 180, 181.

[3] There is historical evidence indicating that the Church's position on jewelry was also controversial for some Adventists during the late 1800's; see, Garry Land, "Adventists in Plain Dress," *Spectrum* 20.2 (1989):42-48. This situation was addressed several times by E. G. White (e.g. *Evangelism*, p. 270).

out to serve as soldiers. It was a constant reminder of their love-commitment to each other.[1] At that time the church in North America was not yet ready to modify its position against the wedding band. During the 1960s some in the church defended the traditional position arguing that society should not determine the standards for the Christian life and that there are standards that will never change. There was also the concern that church members would go beyond the simple wedding band and begin wearing purely ornamental and decorative jewelry.[2]

The increased use of the wedding band among Adventists was of concern to evangelists who were teaching the standard on jewelry to new converts while some church members were not supporting it.[3] The issue of the wedding ring became so intense that during the 1972 Annual Council the church decided to reaffirm and clarify its position on this issue.[4] The resolution acknowledged that although "the quality of an individual's Christianity cannot be gauged solely by external criteria, we do know that his outward appearance will reveal either conformity to the world or to the Word." It called for Church members to apply the principles of self-denial, economy, and simplicity "to all areas of life–to our persons, our homes, our churches, and our institutions." On the specific topic of jewelry it was voted that "in the area of personal adornment necklaces, earrings, bracelets, jeweled and other ornamental rings should not be worn. Articles such as ornamental watches, brooches, cufflinks, etc., should be chosen in harmony with the Christian principles of simplicity, modesty and economy."

The document recognized a close connection between religious convictions and external behavior and appearance. It accepted as implicit the concept that true religion is not only a matter of concepts and ideas but of a dynamic that touches the daily life of the individual. The principles employed to support the standard against jewelry were then used to regulate other aspects in the life of the individual; in fact, they were extended to all areas of life. Interestingly, the statement makes an important distinction between

---

[1]This was the opinion of James R. McCarthy, *Rings Through the Ages* (New York, NY: Harper & Brothers , 1945), p. 182.

[2]R. R. Bietz, "Jewelry–Yesterday and Today," *Review and Herald*, April 21, 1966, pp. 2-3, 9-10. See also, D. A. Delafield, "Ornaments and Jewelry," *Review and Herald*, November 30, 1972, pp. 6,7.

[3]This concern with the lack of support from church members was expressed by Joe Crews, *Colorful Cosmetics and Jewelry* (Frederick, MD: Amazing Facts, 1970).

[4]"Recommendations of General Interest From the Autumn Council 1972-1," *Review and Herald*, November 30, 1972, p. 16. See Appendix I for the full text of the resolution and the vote.

jewelry used for ornamental purpose and jewelry that is of a functional nature and can be worn by believers as long as it is simple, modest and economical. By rejecting "ornamental rings" the church was recognizing that the wedding ring was not necessarily classified as ornamental jewelry.

In a sense there was nothing fundamentally new in the vote taken because the Church had already recognized that the wedding band was considered by Adventists in many places around the world not to be ornamental jewelry. But this official recognition made it possible for the Church in North America to re-evaluate its position on the wedding ring. A few months before the 1972 Annual Council the General Conference officers gave counsel regarding the wedding band in North America. Among other things it was suggested that ministers should not perform ring ceremonies; candidates for baptism were to be encouraged to examine their motives for wearing their wedding ring; baptism was not to be denied to them for wearing it; and Church workers and their families were to be encouraged not to wear the wedding band.[1] The document discouraged the use of the ring but did not condemn it as being in opposition to the standard of the church. Nevertheless, it maintained that "the wearing of the wedding band still is not regarded as obligatory or an imperative custom in North America."[2]

However, certain Adventists were fully persuaded that the social situation had changed in North America and that E. G. White's statement concerning the use of the wedding ring in this country was no longer applicable. They argued that, "Whatever the practice may have been in the past, there is little doubt that the practice of wearing a wedding ring in America today is just as socially imperative as it is in many countries where wearing was permitted by Mrs. White."[3] This change was not considered to be a repudiation of her teaching, rather a reassessment of the present cultural situation in America. But this did not satisfy all in the church and reactions against the wedding band still were heard.[4]

---

[1]See the document, "Counsel Regarding the Wedding Band in North America," GC Officers Meeting, October 2, 1973, p. 72-410.

[2]"Counsel Regarding," p. 72.410.

[3]Roland Churchman, "The Wedding Ring," *Spectrum* 6.1-2 (1974):74.

[4]E.g., S. L. Folkenberg, "Letters from the Readers," *Spectrum* 7.3 (1975):61, 62. He argued that since the practice of wearing a wedding ring was of pagan origin, it should not be followed by Christians.

To defend the use of the wedding ring some suggested that the Adventist rejection of jewelry for personal adornment was not solidly based on the Bible. Passages of Scripture where the use of jewelry was considered acceptable were quoted. For instance, Abraham's servant gave Rebekah bracelets and earrings (Gen 24:22, 53), and the father of the prodigal son gave him a ring (Luke 15:22).[1] Paul's statement in 1 Tim 2:9 was reinterpreted to mean that he "was only reminding women that, in the eyes of God, what counts is one's inner character, not the outer adornment" and that it was not a flat prohibition.[2] The writer, Roland Churchman, emphasized the principles present in the passage and placed little or no emphasis on the explicit mention of jewelry.[3] Meanwhile the Church continued to teach its standard against ornamental jewelry.[4]

During the North American Division 1986 Year-end Meeting, it was considered necessary to make a statement clarifying the position of the Church on the subject of jewelry. The action voted to reaffirm the principles of personal adornment as found in the *Church Manual*, and to recognize that "in harmony with the position stated in the *Church Manual* (pp. 145, 146), some church members in the North American Division as in other

---

[1]Churchman, "Ring," p. 75.

[2]Ibid., p. 76. This same conclusion was reached by C. G. Tuland, "Let's Stop Arguing Over the Wedding Ring," *Spectrum* 8.2 (1977):59. He states that Paul and Peter "do not *prohibit* the braiding of hair, the use of wedding rings or ornaments and the wearing of garments but merely stressed the necessary change from the former pagan outward adornment to the Christian ideal of a changed, spiritual character." He concludes by saying, "We have quoted Scripture only to discover that our interpretation failed in hermeneutical principles and the Bible does not support our position" (p. 81). This line of argumentation would be used and developed even more during the next two decades.

[3]Dan Fahrbach, "God's Jewels," *Insight*, August 1983, pp. 14, 15, uses this approach, but seems to argue against external adornment on the basis that it is our pride and selfishness that makes jewelry inappropriate for Christians. In other words, jewelry is not evil, after all God loves it, but we misuse it.

[4]See R. E. Francis with George E. Vandeman, *God Believes in Jewelry* (Boise, ID: Pacific Press, 1984). They give five reasons for not wearing jewelry: (1) Jesus is our example and he did not wear jewelry; (2) what we do has a positive or negative influence upon others; (3) in the Bible jewelry and consecration to the Lord seem to be incompatible; (4) God's people are compared to a woman without jewelry and God's enemies to a woman with gold ornaments (Rev 12 and 17); Aaron represented God's people during the day of atonement as he officiated dressed with a white linen robe; (5) at the second coming jewelry will not be translated with us, therefore there is no reason to wear it now. His comparison between the attire free of jewelry worn by the high priest during the day of atonement and God's people today has been further developed as a suggestion by Richard M. Davidson, "The Good News of Yom Kippur," *Journal of the Adventist Theological Society* 2.2 (1991):17-18; and Robert J. Wieland, "Jewelry: Shall We Begin Wearing It?" *1888 Message Newsletter* 13.3 (May-July 1997):5-7. It would appear to be quite difficult to develop this kind of typological application from the text itself. During that day the people also rested and, most probably, fasted, but it is impossible to apply this typological approach to those practices. For an evaluation of that suggestion see Samuele Bacchiocchi, *Christian Dress and Adornment* (Berrien Springs, MI: Biblical Perspectives, 1995), pp. 39-41; and George R. Knight, "Proving More than Intended," *Ministry*, March 1996, p. 26.

parts of the world feel that wearing a simple marriage band is a symbol of faithfulness to the marriage vow and to declare that such persons should be fully accepted in the fellowship and service of the church."[1]

One of the factors that led to this change of view was the change of attitude in American society toward the wedding ring which now was being viewed as a symbol of a loving commitment to one's spouse. But the critical factor was a different one. The North American church was receiving many Adventists from overseas divisions, who came to study or to stay, wearing their wedding rings because in their countries the Adventist church had followed the counsel given by E. G. White and the *Church Manual*. With the clash of custom the need rose for the church to clarify its position on this issue.[2] It was this adjustment that the 1972 Annual Council and the 1986 Year-end Meeting of the North American Division did. This could have settled the issue of the wedding ring in North America, but that has not been the case. Many members strongly believe that in America the wedding band is totally unnecessary and have chosen not to wear it.[3] But among others the question is no longer the wedding ring but has become the church's standard against ornamental jewelry.

C. Controversy over the Standard on Jewelry

The biblical validity and relevance of the Adventist position against ornamental jewelry had been an incipient concern among some, but during the last part of the 1980s and throughout the 90s, it became a subject of open and challenging discussion. For the first time in its history the church was confronted by Adventist theologians, sociologists, and other church members who considered the standard–but not the principles behind it–to lack biblical support and to be a remnant of the Victorian age. At least three elements contributed to this shift. First, and perhaps one of the most important, a study on the attitude of Adventist young people toward the standards of the church indicated that, with respect to the specific standard on jewelry, only 39%

---

[1]"Jewelry–A Clarification and Appeal: An Action Voted at the North American Division 1986 Year-end Meeting," *Adventist Review*, August 4, 1988, p. 15. The full text is found in Appendix II.

[2]See, "North America Adopts Adornment Action," *Adventist Review*, December 4, 1986, pp. 9, 10; and Calvin B. Rock, "The Wedding Ring," *Adventist Review*, August 4, 1988, pp. 14, 15.

[3]See, Roger W. Coon, "The Wedding Band, Ellen G. White, and the Seventh-day Adventist Church," unpublished paper, 1987. Some church members tended to believe that the church erred by accepting the wedding band; see Calvin B. Rock's answer to a question on this subject by a church elder in "Faith Alive! Gems and Jewels," *Adventist Review*, October 24, 1996, p. 29; cf. Bacchiocchi, *Adornment*, pp. 102-138.

agreed with the position of the church, while 42% disagreed.[1] The results of the study suggested that the church should give immediate attention to the issue of Christian standards. The subject became so important that the *Ministry* magazine dedicated the entire issue of October 1989 to explore it and soon a book-length report was published by the Valugenesis study group to address it.[2] Several articles were written on this important subject. In one of them Gerald Wheeler traced the history of Adventist standards, arguing that the Methodist background of our pioneers determined the position of the church on some of the issues but in the process it developed its own identity. Sociological factors were used to explain the foundation of the standards suggesting at the same time that as society changes we must be willing to re-examine them and perhaps add new ones.[3]

David Newman suggested that there are three level of standards: absolutes, that never change and are always valid (the Ten Commandments); temporal, that is to say they are required for the people of God everywhere but have limited temporal existence (e.g., circumcision ended with the cross; baptism by immersion ends at the Second Coming); and cultural standards

---

[1]See, Janet Leigh Kangas and Roger L. Dudley, "How Adventist Teenagers Perceive their Church," *Ministry*, October 1989, pp. 4-7; Roger L. Dudley with V. Bailey Gillespie, *Faith in the Balance* (Riverside, CA: La Sierra University Press, 1992), pp. 49, 148. We must point out that the studies prepared in response to those statistical findings paid little attention to the fact that almost half of the young people supported the standard of the church on ornamental jewelry.

[2]Steve Case, ed., *Valuegenesis: Shall We Dance–Rediscovering Christ Centered Standards* (Riverside, CA: La Sierra University Press, 1996).

[3]Gerald Wheeler, "The Historical Basis of Adventist Standards," *Ministry*, October 1989, pp. 8-12. One cannot deny that social practices play a role in defining standards, but it is not enough for the Christian to establish them by selecting "from culture what is timeless and useful" (p. 10). We do have biblical passages, cases and stories that illustrate how principles functioned in the life of the individual in biblical times and we must pay attention to them. Caleb Rosado has forcefully argued for the strong influence of culture on our reading and interpretation of the Bible ("Thinking About Standards: Social Conditioning Reality," *Shall We Dance*, pp. 32-39). That influence cannot be totally denied, but we also have to allow for the work of the Spirit in assisting us in gaining a true knowledge of God and His will for based on the Bible and that are not culturally determined. I suspect that even though Rosado and Wheeler seem to be over stressing social conditioning and social relativism, they will probably recognize the limitations of that approach. Steve Case is a little more radical when he states, "Although it is possible for some applications of principles to remain the same from generation to generation and from culture to culture, we should not expect that to be the case, especially in a pluralistic society in which change seems to be the constant" ("Thinking About Standards: Basic Considerations," *Shall We Dance*, p. 40; a similar view is taken by Dennis H. Braun, "A Seminar on Adventists, Adornment and Jewelry," D. Min. Project Report, Andrews University, 1996, pp. 65-67). This position seems extreme. An example could illustrate the problem. One could argue that the principle of physical and spiritual rest leads to the specific standard that no work is to be done during the *seventh day of the week*. Should not the principle *and the standard* remain valid across time and culture?

whose main concern is with local or universal practices (e.g., preaching with a coat on, dress style, adornments).[1]

The discussion on standards seemed designed to show that standards are strongly influenced by social practices and they do need revisions. If they are no longer relevant, as suggested by the negative attitude of young people toward some of them, then, it was argued, revisions are necessary. What about ornamental jewelry? Is this a culturally conditioned standard? Those studies implicitly suggested so.

A second element that shifted discussion from the wedding ring to ornamental jewelry was the realization that the standard appeared to be inconsistent in its application in real life. This was not new,[2] but now this argument was reinforced to question the position of the church.[3] The following quote illustrates the problem: "What about a tiny earring? In official teaching this is a forbidden item of apparel. But if I attach it to my tie, then it's a tie clasp. Attaching it to a woman's suit, of course, makes it a brooch. Either way, it suddenly belongs to the category of what can be worn. It's simple transformation, but also a puzzling one-as is this whole topic."[4]

The inconsistencies extend to other areas. For instance, jewelry is rejected

---

[1]J. David Newman, "Standards Define Relationships," *Ministry*, October 1989, pp. 18-21. He defines principles "as universal rules, usually given in the abstract, such as courtesy, obedience, love, equality. Standards are specific applications of these principles. While principles cross all cultural barriers, standards very from culture to culture except for 10 important exceptions [Ten Commandments]" (p. 18). His definition of standard appears to exclude his second level of standards because, according to his own understanding, standards under that level are valid for God's people everywhere and, therefore, in every culture. Another question is the extent to which it is right to refer to the Ten Commandments as standards and not principles. In some cases they seem to be a combination of both, e.g. the Sabbath commandment. Newman also pointed out that the rejection of ornamental jewelry is usually considered a *requirement to become a member of the church* and yet it is not listed as such in the 27 fundamental beliefs or in the *Church Manual* (p. 20). This is indeed an interesting phenomenon and perhaps it indicates that since the church considers it to be a biblical standard it is authoritative by itself.

My reading of materials produced by Adventists on the topic of principles and standards suggests to me that there is not a clear understanding of what a standard is and how it is established. Each writer seems to have his or her own working definition. For instance, as indicated above, some believe that standards are determined to a large extent by culture and others consider them to be largely subjective (James Coffin, "The Standard Problem," *Adventist Review*, June 9, 1998, p. 5). None of them has seriously attempted to clarify what is a *biblical* standard. In this work a biblical standard is a specific rule of life whose authority is dependent on the teachings of the Bible.

[2]See for instance, Frances Mohr, "Where is Our Consistency?" *Review and Herald*, April 8, 1971, p. 11.

[3]Charles Scriven, "'I Didn't Recognize You With Your Ring On,'" *Spectrum* 20.2 (1989):56-59.

[4]Ibid., p. 57.

on the basis of the principles of economy and modesty, but nothing is said about expensive watches, cars, houses, etc.

It is useful to have scholars pointing to the broad applications of biblical principles dealing with Christian lifestyle. The problem of inconsistency is a real one and some have suggested that the way to solve it is by making "an exhaustive list or have no list and teach just the principles."[1] Making an exhaustive list is neither possible[2] nor desirable because it would lead to legalism. What is suggested then, is to work on the basis of principles. The fundamental principle is, according to them, simplicity in life-style.[3] In other words, the suggestion is that church members, and not the church, should decide by themselves which type of ornamental jewelry expresses the biblical principle of simplicity in adornment.[4] Of course this suggestion is valid only if the biblical materials on jewelry can be shown to be promoting a principle and not a specific standard valid across time and culture.

The third element that contributed to the shift under discussion was the realization by some that the biblical passages used by the church to support its position on the standard against ornamental jewelry have been misinterpreted.[5] Read in their contexts, it is suggested, those passages are promoting the principle of modesty in dress and the reference to specific pieces of jewelry was based on the significance they had in biblical times

---

[1]Newman, "Relationships," p. 21.

[2]J. David Newman, "Raising or Lowering the Standards?" *Ministry*, December 1992, pp. 6-7, comments that not even the Bible provides a complete list of what is and is not appropriate.

[3]Scriven, "Your Ring," pp. 58,59.

[4]Cf. Steve Case, "Basic Considerations," p. 41. Obviously, there is nothing wrong with promoting simplicity in lifestyle. William G. Johnsson wrote an editorial on the subject of simplicity in which he combined this principle and the church's standard on jewelry ("On Behalf of Simplicity," *Adventist Review*, March 20, 1986, p. 4). We must recognize the contribution made by those who have addressed the topic of biblical principles and church standards. They have explored the many biblical principles involved on the issue of lifestyle and are challenging our young people to live up to those principles. They do believe that there are certain types of jewelry, cars, houses, etc., that are incompatible with some basic Christian principles. For a discussion of those principles see, Steve Case, "Thinking About Standards: Ground Rules for Discussion," *Shall We Dance*, pp. 47-53; Gary Russell, "Thinking About Jewelry: Looking at the Outward Appearance," Ibid., pp. 195-203; Steve Chavez, "Thinking About Jewelry: Because We are Adventists," Ibid., pp. 204-207; Dick Duerksen, "Thinking About Jewelry: Jewelry and Spiritual Experience," Ibid., pp. 214-216; and Dennis H. Braun, "Adventists, Adornment and Jewelry," pp. 70-77. Particularly useful is Monte Sahlin, "Church Standards Today: Where are We Going?" *Ministry*, October 1989, pp. 13-17. Perhaps a better understanding of the nature and role of jewelry in the Bible could assist all of us in bridging the gap between principle and a specific standard on jewelry.

[5]See particularly, Madelyn Jones-Hadelman, "Adorning the Temple of God," Spectrum 20.2 (1989):51-55; and Steve Case, "Thinking About Jewelry: What the Bible (Really) Says," in *Shall We Dance*, pp.184-193.

and culture. In addition it is stated that there is no prohibition against jewelry in the Old Testament or evidence indicating that the Israelites were not to adorn themselves with jewelry. Here we arrive at a fundamental question: What does the Bible actually teach concerning the use of jewelry? The sociology of jewelry is important, but for an Adventist the fundamental issue is the one of the will of God. If those who question the position of the church are right then the church must listen carefully.

Some have joined the discussion on the topic of jewelry to argue that the Adventist understanding of the biblical texts on this subject is exegetically sound. Samuele Bacchiochi's book on the subjects of dress and adornment not only deal with the biblical texts but also with the biblical principles behind them and the history of those standards.[1] He seems to conclude that the Bible rejects the use of any type of jewelry by God's people. This claim should be carefully analyzed. The need for church standards on Christian lifestyle has been voiced by Jay Gallimore who has also alerted us to the legalistic use of these standards and to the more permissive attitude of letting people do whatever they feel is right. He concludes that church standards are the minimum God requires from us, not the maximum.[2]

Sandra Doran has suggested that the Adventist position on jewelry frees women from the slavery of jewel ornaments imposed on them by society.[3] She adds that "all organizations have the right to establish standards based on their mission" and invites church leaders to hold up the standard in their own lives.[4] Erik Stenbakken puts the emphasis on using fundamental principles to govern our lives without rejecting the biblical understanding of personal adornment because it embodies the principle of true value.[5] In

---

[1] Samuele Bacchiochi, *Christian Dress and Adornment* (Berrien Springs, MI: Biblical Perspectives, 1995), pp. 50, 71.

[2] Jay Gallimore, "Christian Standards: Minimums, Not Maximums," *Adventist Review*, December 3, 1992, pp. 8-11.

[3] Sandra Doran, "Dialogues: Judged Valuable," *Adventist Review*, April 18, 1996, p. 15. For an Adventist appraisal of the enslaving power of society on the way we look, see Gary Krause, "Dying for an Image," *Adventist Review*, August 21, 1997, pp. 8-12.

[4] Ibid. This contradicts the opinion of Steve Daily, *Adventism for a New Generation* (Portland, OR: Better Living Publishers, 1993), p. 20, where he states, "It is not the business of the church to prescribe for its members how they should behave on Sabbath, what foods they should eat, in what forms of recreation or entertainment they may participate, what books they can read, how they should dress, if they can wear jewelry, or how they should think." This radical position tends to make it impossible to incorporate him in any productive dialogue on this subject.

[5] Erik Stenbakken, "The Issue Is Value," *Adventist Review*, June 19, 1997, pp. 12-14.

the same vein Lesley Kay wrote, "Self-motivated self-improvement is as old as sin. The naked soul blushes with shame at its exposed vulnerability and imperfection, and seeks a thousand ways to hide. I've concluded that wearing jewelry is just one of the ways that human nature compulsively attempts to cover its nakedness and validate itself by asserting, 'I'm attractive; I'm worthwhile; I'm a person of substance.'"[1] These writers believe that the Adventist standard on jewelry is biblical, based on solid principles, and has positive spiritual, psychological, and sociological benefits. Meanwhile, the church continues to affirm throughout the world its principles and standards on Christian behavior.[2]

D. Conclusion

Our journey through recent Adventist literature on the subject of jewelry reveals that at the present time there is strong support for the position of the church, paralleled by significant opposition. The fundamental issue confronting the church today on the subject is its alleged lack of biblical support. The argument is that the proof-text method used to support it is no longer valid because each passage must be analyzed within its own context and in terms of the writer's intention. This concern has merit and should be taken seriously by all of us who claim to base our beliefs and practices on the Bible.

Traditionally we have employed a limited set of biblical passages to support our position on jewelry (e.g., Isa 3:16-26; 1 Tim 2:9,10; 1 Pet 3:1-6), but have not examined a significant number of other passages dealing with this same subject. A number of those passages could give the impression to some readers that wearing jewelry is not necessarily wrong. Consequently, some of our sincere church members have been confused and when seeking answers from church workers the responses, at least in some cases, were not satisfactory. Therefore, it is indispensable for us to look at the biblical materials.

---

[1]Leslie Kay, "On the Home Front: This Jewelry Thing," *Adventist Review*, August 1998, p. 28. Charles D. Brooks, "Answers," Message, November-December 1994, p. 14, had already pointed to the biblical stand on jewelry as a call to humility and the rejection of self-centeredness.

[2]This is particularly being done through the influential book, *Seventh-day Adventists Believe. . ..: A Biblical Exposition of 27 Fundamental Doctrines* (Hagerstown, MD: Review and Herald, 1988), pp. 278-292.

JEWELRY IN THE OT:
A DESCRIPTION OF ITS FUNCTION[1]

A. Introduction

The Old Testament uses a variety of terms to designate different types of ornaments. There are references to ornaments in general (e.g. Prov 25:12), fibulas, earrings, rings, ornaments for the neck and breast of a woman (Exod 35:22), ear pendants (Judges 6:26), anklets (Prov 7:22), bracelet (Gen 24:22), necklace (Ezek 16:1), and others. In many cases the meaning of the Hebrew terms used to designate specific ornaments is unknown and translators are forced to guess. The biblical evidence, archaeological findings, ancient iconography, literary works and inscriptions indicate that the use of jewelry was very common throughout the ancient Near East and played a significant role in those societies.

In this chapter we will catalogue the usage of jewelry in the Old Testament, indicating at times its parallels with ancient Near Eastern practices. This is an area of study in which one can find elements of continuity and discontinuity between Israel and its neighbors and between Israel's official religion and popular practices. We will show that jewelry was a vehicle for the expression of cultural, social, religious and magical practices and convictions. In a sense it was a concrete expression of the individual's interests, values, concerns and fears, and of his or her standing in society. However, our main interest is to explore the Old Testament's attitude toward that phenomenon.

B. Uses of Jewelry in the Old Testament[2]
1. Used as Adornment

Personal adornment is the most obvious purpose of jewelry in the ancient Near East, as evidenced in part by the simple fact that in general it was beautifully crafted and, therefore, it served to enhance the appearance

---

[1]This is a revised version of my article, "Jewelry in the Old Testament: A Description of Its Function," in *To Understand the Scriptures: Essays in Honor of William Shea*, edited by David Merling (Berrien Springs, MI: Institute of Archaeology, 1997), pp. 103-124.

[2]Probably one of the best sources of drawings depicting jewelry from the ancient Near East is the book by K. R. Maxwell-Hyslop, *Western Asiatic Jewelry c. 3000-612 B.C.* (London: Methuen, 1971).

of the individual wearing it.[1] One of the best examples of this function of jewelry in the OT is found in the dress of the High Priest which was decked with precious and semi-precious stones and gold. It is explicitly stated that one of the basic purposes of this special and unique attire was to beautify (*tiph'eret*) this religious leader (Exod 28:2). The noun *tiph'eret* seems to emphasize that which makes people feel happy and proud[2] and can be rendered "ornament, splendor, beauty." The negative side of this picture is recorded in Isa 3:16-23 where Israelite ladies put on their jewelry to beautify themselves attracting attention to their own proud persons. The catalogue is introduced by the term *tiph'eret*, indicating that the elements listed were considered to be beautiful.[3]

In Ezekiel's allegory of Jerusalem the city is compared to a beautiful girl adorned with different kinds of jewelry (16:11-15). This time the verb used, *yph* ("become beautiful"), tends to put the stress on the attractiveness of outward appearance,[4] which in this particular case is directly associated with jewelry. In Ezek 23:40 God's people are likened to a woman who painted her eyes and adorned herself with ornaments in order to improve her appearance and to increase her sex-appeal.[5] The same idea is expressed in Jer 4:30 and clearly indicates that Israel

---

[1]In an old Babylonian letter a son writes to his father asking him to send him "a fine string full of beads, to be worn around the head . . . It should be full (of beads) and should be beautiful. If I see it and dislike (?) it, I shall send it back!" (A. Leo Oppenheim, *Letters from Mesopotamia* [Chicago, IL: University of Chicago Press, 1967], p. 87). On the use and symbolism of beads consult, Sally Dunham, "Beads for Babies," *Zeitschrift für Assyriologie und Vorderasiatische Archäologie* 83 (1993):237-57. For a study of the manufacture of beads see, A. John Gwinnett and Leonard Gorelick, "Bead Manufacture at Hajar ar-Rayhani, Yemen," *Biblical Arachaeologist* 54 (1991):187-96.

[2]See, D. Vetter, "P'r," in *Theologisches Handworterbuch zum Alten Testament*, vol. 2, Ernst Jenni and Claus Westermann, eds. (Munich: Kaiser, 1971), 2:387 (hereafter THAT).

[3]Cf. Elizabeth Ellen Platt, "Jewelry of Bible Times and the Catalog of Isa 3:18-23: Part I," *Andrews University Seminary Studies* 17 (1979):71-73.

[4]Cf. Helmer Ringgren, *"Yapah,"* in *Theological Dictionary of the OT*, eds. G. J. Botterweck and Helmer Ringgren, vol. 6 (Grand Rapids, MI: Eerdmans, 1990), p. 219.

[5]Prostitutes wore jewelry in order to look more attractive (Hosea 2:2 [4], 13 [15]; cf. Rev 17:4, 5); see, Elaine Adler Goodfriend, ""Prostitution (OT)," *Anchor Bible Dictionary, vol. 5*, edited by David Noel Freedman (New York, NY: Doubleday, 1992), pp. 506-07. For an example from the ancient Near East see, Theophile J. Meek, "Middle Assyrian Laws, 40," *Ancient Near Eastern Texts Relating to the OT*, James B. Pritchard, ed. (Princeton, NJ: Princeton University Press, 1969), p.183. On the use of cosmetics in the ancient world see, R. J. Forbes, *Studies in Ancient Technology*, vol. 3 (Leiden: Brill, 1965), pp. 1-50; and E. Cassin, "Kosmetik," *Reallexikon der Assyriologie* 6 (1981):214-18.

was attempting to make herself beautiful.[1] The description is similar to the experience of Jezebel before she was killed (2 Kings 9:30).

The OT recognizes the beauty of gold, silver and precious stones. In the Song of Songs the arms of the beloved are described as "rounded gold set with jewels. His body is ivory work, encrusted with sapphires" (5:14). He describes her saying, "Your rounded thighs are like jewels, the work of a master hand" (7:1; cf. Lam 4:7). In both cases the beauty and value of each other is being praised by comparing parts of the body to gold and precious stones. The costliness and beauty of those objects made it possible to use them as "metaphors of positive ethical and spiritual values" (e.g. Prov 25:12; Job 28:18; Prov 3:15; 8:11; 31:10).[2]

In spite of the fact that one of the functions of jewelry was decorative this was not always its exclusive or even primary purpose. Together with its ornamental element we find several other reasons for wearing jewelry.

2. Used as Currency

Before the invention of coinage or money, jewelry was used as a medium of exchange.[3] It appears to have been a common practice through most of the ancient Near East to make pieces of jewelry with a standardized weight which could then be used in commercial transactions in exchange for other goods or as payment for work done.[4] This is the function of the jewelry given by Abraham's servant to Rebekah at the well.

According to the biblical record the servant gave Rebekah a gold ring weighing half shekel and a pair of bracelets weighing ten gold shekels (Gen 24:22). Two elements in the narrative suggest that this jewelry was given to her on account of services rendered. First, he gave her the pieces of

---

[1]The hithpael of the verb *yph* could be translated "try to beautify oneself;" see, William L. Holladay, *Jeremiah 1: A Commentary on the Book of the Prophet Jeremiah Chapters 1-25* (Philadelphia: Fortress, 1986), p. 170.

[2]Malcolm J. A. Horsnell, *"ʿdh,"* *New International Dictionary of OT Theology and Exegesis*, vol. 3, Willem A. VanGemeren, ed. (Grand Rapids, MI: Zondervan, 1997), p. 323.

[3]See, Renate Rosenthal, *Jewellery in Ancient Times* (London: Cassell, 1973), p. 7. We find this practice also at Ebla; see, Alfonso Archi, "Gifts for a Prince," in *Eblatica: Essays on the Ebla Archives and Eblaite Language,* Cyrus H. Gordon; Gary A. Rendsburg; and Nathan H. Winter, eds. (Winona Lake, IL: Eisenbrauns, 1987), pp. 116-17; *idem.,* "Circulation d'objets en metal précieux de poids standardisé a Ebla," in *Miscellanea Babylonica: Mélanges offerts a Maurice Birot,* J.-R. Kupper, ed. (Paris: Editions Recherche, 1985), pp. 25-33.

[4]For instance, in Egypt, during the Old Kingdom, working women were usually paid in jewelry (Henry G. Fischer, "Women in the Old Kingdom and the Heracleopolitan Period," in *Women's Earliest Records From Ancient Egypt and Western Asia,* Barbara S. Lesko, ed. [Atlanta, GA: Scholars, 1989], p. 16). Jewelry was also used, among other places, in Egypt (*Ancient Near Eastern Texts,* p. 18) and in Assyria (Ibid., p. 275) to pay tributes.

jewelry only after she performed a valuable service for him and his animals. Not only did she provide water for Abraham's servant and his men (vs. 22), but also for their ten camels! Unquestionably, that was quite a task that required from her much effort and energy.[1] The gold given to her was her reward for a task well done.[2] Second, it is important to notice that the narrative indicates the weight of the jewelry. This piece of information "is due to the fact that such items were cast according to fixed standards and used as media of exchange."[3] The amount paid may seem to be too high but this could be explained by suggesting that the servant already suspected that this was the woman God had chosen for Isaac. The fact that jewelry was considered "money" did not hinder the person from wearing it; Rebekah put it on her person. It may well be that in some cases people went out to do business transaction literally wearing their "money." We would, then, have a merging of two different functions of jewelry, namely, adornment and currency.

3. Evidence of Wealth

Jewelry was used to indicate the economical or financial well-being of a person (cf. 2 Chr 32:27; 1 Kgs 10:2). Abraham was a wealthy individual not only because he had servants and many animals but also because he had silver and gold (Gen 24:35). These precious metals were preserved in the form of jewelry (vss. 10, 22). The bridewealth usually included jewelry[4] and

---

[1]This was also observed by, Bruce Vawter, *On Genesis: A New Reading* (Garden City, NY: Doubleday, 1977), p. 269. Unfortunately he argues that the gifts were part of the bride price. The same is the case of Victor P. Hamilton, *The Book of Genesis: Chapters 18-50* (Grand Rapids, MI: Eerdmans, 1995), p. 148; and Elizabeth E. Platt, "Jewelry, Ancient Israel," in *Anchor Bible Dictionary*, vol. 3, p. 826.

[2]Gordon J. Wenham, *Genesis 15-50* (Dallas, TX: Word, 1994), p. 145. According to C. Westermann, *Genesis 12-36: A Commentary* (Minneapolis: Augsburg, 1985), p. 387, the jewelry given by the servant to the girl was "nothing other than his joyful reaction to the girls's obliging readiness to refresh him and his animals (not some sort of bride price!)." For a comparison with ancient Near Eastern practices see, M. Anbar, "Les bijoux compris dans la dot du fiancé a Mari e dans les cadeaux du mariage dans Gn. 24," *Ugarit-Forschungen* 6 (1974):442-44.

[3]Nahum M. Sarna, *Genesis* (Philadelphia: Jewish Publications, 1989), p. 165.

[4]See, Maxwell-Hyslop, *Jewelry*, pp. 135-36. On questions related to the concepts and practice of dowry, brideprice and bridewealth in the ancient Near East, consult, Katarzyna Grosz, "Dowry and Brideprice in Nuzi," in *Studies on the Civilization and Culture of Nuzi and Hurrians*, M. A. Morrison and D. I. Owen, eds. (Winona Lake, IN: Eisenbraun, 1981), pp.161-82; *Idem.*, "Bridewealth and Dowry in Nuzi," in *Images of Women in Antiquity*, Averil Cameron and Amélie Kuhrt, eds. (Detroit, MI: Wayne State University Press, 1983), pp. 193-206; Martha T. Roth, *Babylonian Marriage Agreements Seventh-Third Centuries B. C.* (Neukirchen-Vlyun: Neukirchener Verlag, 1984), pp. 7-10; idem., "Marriage and Matrimonial Prestations in First Millennium B. C. Babylonia," in *Women's Earliest Records*, ed. Barbara S. Lesko (Atlanta, GA: Scholars), pp. 245-55; Samuel Greengus, "Bridewealth in Sumerian Sources," *Hebrew Union College Annual* 61 (1990):25-88; and Maria Giovanna Biga, "Femmes de la famille royale d'Ebla," in *La femme dans le proche-orient antique*, Jean-Marie Durand, ed. (Paris: Editions Recherches, 1987), pp.41-47.

in the case of Abraham's servant this was clearly the case. After the family decided to allow Rebekah to go with him he gave her a gift as a bridewealth: "The servant brought forth jewelry [*kᵉlê*] of silver and of gold, and raiment, and gave them to Rebekah" (vs. 53). The term *kᵉlî* could designate gold and silver utensils but it is also used to designate jewelry.[1] In this particular case it was a gift to the bride to ensure her future financial security. It would appear that it was the custom for the bride to put on this jewelry during the wedding ceremony to beautify herself and display her wealth (Jer 2:32; Isa 49:18; 61:10). Another example of this practice is found in Ezek 16, where Israel is represented by a young adolescent girl whom the Lord is going to marry, to make His queen. He gives her a bridewealth consisting of bracelets, necklace, nose ring, etc. Later she abandoned Him, took her bridewealth with her and spent it with her lovers (16:33) and whatever was left of it her lovers removed from her (16:39), leaving her in poverty.

Shortly before the exodus from Egypt God ordered the Israelites to "ask, every man from his neighbor, and every woman of her neighbor, jewelry of silver and of gold"(Exod 11:2). This request has been interpreted in different ways,[2] but the use of the verb *nasal* ("to plunder"), in 12:36, provides the basic theological reason for it. The exodus from Egypt appears to be depicted here as a military defeat over the Egyptians and their gods (12:12, 41) and the spoils belonged to the victorious ones, the Israelites (2 Chr 20:25). The fundamental theological concern of the narrative "focuses on God's plan for the Israelites to leave Egypt as victors from a battle."[3] Jewelry (*kᵉlî*) was part of the spoils and the defeated ones handed it over to the Israelites voluntarily thus enriching them. This seems to be described as a fulfillment of the promise God made to Abraham that his descendants will leave Egypt "with great possessions" (Gen 15:14). The Lord made sure that they left Egypt with

---

[1]See, K.-M. Beyse, "*Keli*," *Theological Dictionary of the OT*, vol. 7, pp. 172-73.

[2]Among them we find the following ones: (1) an example of the Israelite law concerning the emancipation of slaves, cf. Deut 15:13 (e. g. Walter C. Kaiser, Jr., "Exodus," in *The Expositor's Bible Commentary*, vol 2, Frank E. Gaebelin, ed. [Grand Rapids, MI: Zondervan, 1990], p. 323); (2) the gifts "represent the equivalent of the income the Israelites ought to have received over the years as a living wage " (George A. F. Knight, *Theology as Narration: A Commentary on the Book of Exodus* [Grand Rapids, MI: Eerdmans, 1976], p. 27); (3) a literary detail used "to explain how it came about later that the Israelites in the wilderness were able to erect a sanctuary and to furnish it with all kinds of precious materials" (Nahum M. Sarna, *Exploring Exodus* [New York: Schocken, 1986], p. 57). These three explanations are not necessarily mutually exclusive and may represent different elements present in the request.

[3]Brevard S. Child, *The Book of Exodus* (Philadelphia: Westminster, 1974), pp. 176-77. A similar position was taken by R. Alan Cole, Exodus (Downers Grove, IL: Inter-Varsity, 1973), p. 67; and John I. Durham, *Exodus* (Waco, TX: Word, 1987), pp. 40, 147.

a firm financial base as they began a new life in their journey toward the promised land. The primary purpose of jewelry in this narrative is to provide some financial security to the Israelites. Interestingly, the people were instructed to place the jewelry on their sons and daughters (Exod 3:22). If by this is meant that they wore it, then we can suggest that they were to display the spoils of war, the acquired wealth of their parents.[1]

4. Symbol of Social Status

Jewelry functioned as an identifying mark of the individual's position in the social strata and his or her role within it. This is one of the most common uses of jewelry in the OT. The figure of the king is probably the most important one in this respect.[2] Saul wore a crown ($n\bar{e}zer$) and an armlet ('$es'\bar{a}\,d\bar{a}h$; 2 Sam 1:10) as his royal insignia. The "crown" could have been of metal or silk, it may have been adorned with jewels (Zech 9:16), and was used by Israelites kings (2 Kings 11:12; Pss 21:3; 89:39 [40]; 132:18).[3] Armlets and bracelets were particularly worn by royal figures in the ancient Near East.[4] In this passage these two adornments serve the primary function of defining the social function of Saul, the king of Israel.[5]

The oracle against the king of Tyre in Ezekiel 28:11-19 contains references to jewelry which can be interpreted primarily as signifying royal status. This oracle is difficult to interpret because in its description of the evilness of the king the prophet uses language which goes far beyond the experience of the literal king of Tyre. He uses the experience of a celestial being and his

---

[1]Platt has argued that the fact that the items were placed on the children may suggest that "these were not large amounts of gold and silver to be carried by adults for use in trade or commercial exchange" ("Jewelry, Ancient Israel," p. 832). But the rest of the exodus narrative does suggest that the amount was considerably significant because some of it was probably used to make the golden calf (32:2-5) and given as offerings for the construction of the tabernacle (35:20-22). Cf. J. P. Hyatt, *Exodus* (Grand Rapids, MI: Eerdmans, 1971), pp. 138, 304. Notice that later on we are told that women were also wearing jewelry (Exod 32:2).

[2]After defeating Neku, Ashurbanipal took him to Nineveh and there he "clothed him in splendid (lit. brightly colored) garments, laid upon his (neck) a golden chain, as the emblem of his royalty. I put rings of gold upon his fingers, gave him an iron girdle dagger, set in gold . . ." (D. D. Luckenbill, *Ancient Records of Assyria and Babylonia*, vol. 2 [Chicago, IL: University Press, 1926-27], p. 295). On the dress of the Pharaoh see, Elisabeth Staehelin, "Ornat," in *Lexikon der Agyptologie*, vol. 4, W. Helck and E. Otto, eds. (Wiesbaden: Harrassowitz, 1981), cols. 613-16.

[3]Cf. W. A. Raffety, "Crown," in *International Standard Bible Encyclopedia*, vol 1, Geoffrey W. Bromiley, ed. (Grand Rapids, MI: Eerdmans, 1979), p. 831.

[4]A. A. Anderson, *2 Samuel* (Dallas, TX: Word, 1989), p. 8.

[5]See, P. Kyle McCarter, Jr., *2 Samuel* (Garden city, NY: Doubleday, 1984), p.60.

fall to illustrate what happened to this earthly king.[1] This being, whom the prophet projects into the person of the king of Tyre and whose activities and attitude he images, is described as decked with many precious stones and wearing a dress embroidered with strings of gold.[2] Since the list of precious stones is very similar to those worn by the High Priest some have concluded that the reference to jewelry has the purpose of identifying him as a priestly figure. But the differences would suggest that the high priestly image is not the primary one in the prophet's mind.[3] It seems better to conclude that the description of his dress has the primary purpose of describing his royal status. He was a prince. Throughout the ancient Near East the vestment of kings were embroidered with precious metals and loaded with precious gems.[4] This does not exclude the use of jewelry as adornment to beautify this prince (28:12).

---

[1]Scholars are still debating the background of Ezekiel's language and imagery in this particular pericope. For details consult, Walther Zimmerli, *Ezekiel 2: A Commentary on the Book of Prophet Ezekiel Chapters 25-48* (Philadelphia: Fortress, 1983), pp. 81-95; and James A. Miller, "The Malak of Tyre (Ezekiel 28,11-19)," *Zeitschrift für die alttestamentliche Wissenschaft* 105 (1993):497-501, who argues that the background is a story about the rebellion of a heavenly kerub. The more common connection suggested by scholars is with the Paradise Story of Genesis, e.g. John L. McKenzie, "Mythological Allusions in Ezek 28:12-18," *Journal of Biblical Literature* 75 (1976):322-27; cf. Carol A. Newsom, "A Maker of Metaphors: Ezekiel's Oracle Against Tyre," *Interpretation* 38 (1984):158-64.

[2]The Hebrew text is not totally clear with respect to the function of the precious stones mentioned in Ezek 28:13. Where they part of the garden or were they adorning this kingly figure? The uncertainty lies in the fact that we do not know the exact meaning of some of the key Hebrew terms used in the text (See, Zimmerli, Ezekiel 2, pp. 82-85; and Leslie C. Allen, *Ezekiel 28-40* [Dallas, TX: Word, 1990], pp. 91, 94). A literal translation of the first part of verse 13 would be: "In Eden, the Garden of God, you were. All precious stones [were] your *mᵉsukah*, ruby, topaz . . ." There is no verb in the second sentence but I supplied the verb "were." The Hebrew term *mᵉsukah* is rendered in most translations as a verb, "adorned you," but it is a noun. Its meaning is uncertain but is usually considered to mean "a cover," in the sense of vestments. In that case the king wears the gems as part of his dress. But it could also designate an enclosure, and in that case the precious stones are part of the surroundings within which the king moved. The stones would be part of the garden. Support for the second interpretation is found in verses 14–"You walked among the fiery stones"–and 16–"I expelled you, O guardian cherub, from among the fiery stones." The usual translation of the last part of verse 13 suggests that the stones adorned the king: "Your settings and mountings [on you] were made of gold; on the day you were created they were prepared." But again we face translation difficulties. The sentence begins with two nouns ("settings and mountings") whose Hebrew meanings are uncertain. The Hebrew *bak* "on you," could also mean "in you," "with you." In other words, whatever the golden objects might be, they were not necessarily on the person of the king but could have been with him as part of his surroundings. Nevertheless, most ancient translations have taken the passage to mean that the kingly figure was adorned with precious stones and that is the prevailing view among scholars. I must say that the text, in spite of the linguistic problems, leans toward that meaning.

[3]P. L. Garber and R. W. Funk, "Jewels and Precious Stones," in *Interpreter's Dictionary of the Bible*, vol. 2, George A. Buttrick, ed. (Nashville, TN: Abingdon, 1962), pp. 903, write, "It is frequently asserted that, in view of Ezekiel's priestly interests, there is in his listing a reflection of the stones of the Exodus high-priest's-breastpiece passage. This is conceivable, yet the smaller total number of stones and the inexact correspondence of the order in which the stones are named raise a question as to any kind of literal or mechanical interdependence of the passages."

[4]See above n. 60, and below n. 127.

The social position of the queen is also indicated by her use of jewelry.[1] Her queenly status is granted to her during her wedding at which time "the princess is decked in her chamber with gold-woven robes; in many-colored robes she is led to the king, with her virgin companions, her escort, in her train" (Ps 45:9, 13,14). This is a colorful description of a wedding ceremony during which the princess "takes her place of honor to the right of the king, adorned with gold of Ophir."[2] It is this social custom that God uses in Ezek 16 to describe the royal status assigned by Him to Jerusalem, her election and her privileges. The chapter is probably an allegory or parable in which Jerusalem is compared to a foundling girl, abandoned by her parents at birth. The Lord found her, cared for her and when she matured into adulthood He married her.[3] As wedding gifts He gave her bracelets, a neck chain, nose ring, earrings, and a crown (16:10-12). Dressed with beautiful garments and decked with jewelry she became the wife of the Lord, His queen (16:13). Her social status embodied itself in the kind of dress and adornment she wore. All of these were symbolic of the glorious status that God bestowed on Jerusalem when He selected it to be His city.[4] The parable goes on to describe how she misused the gift given to her by the Lord and the results of that rebellion.

---

[1]During the wedding of the Sumerian goddess Inanna she "prepared herself to meet Dumuzi as befits a Sumerian queenly bride, washing, anointing and bedecking herself, and not failing to take along her dowry and seal" (S. N. Kramer, "Courting, Marriage, and Honeymoon," in *ANET*, 639). Nabonidus buried his mother dressed like a queen "(clad in) fine woolen garments, shining linen, (with) golden A.LU, precious and costly stones [he decked her out] . . ." (A. Leo Oppenheim, "Babylonian and Assyrian Historical Texts," in *ANET*, p. 312).

[2]Hans-Joachim Kraus, *Psalms 1-59: A Continental Commentary* (Minneapolis: Augsburg, 1988), p. 456. A similar description of the bride of the king adorned with jewelry is found in Song 1:10. It is difficult to know the type of jewelry that some of the Hebrew terms used there designate. Othmar Keel, *The Songs of Song: A Continental Commentary* (Minneapolis: Fortress, 1994), p. 59, gives the following possibilities: "The Hebrew term tôrîm, translated in the NRSV as 'ornaments,' literally means 'rows' (Esth. 2:12, 15), 'bands' (Akkadian), or 'borders' (Aramaic). One must think of a kind of jewelry that sets off the cheeks, similar to the cheek bands on a horse's bridle. Possibilities include dangling earrings, ribbons on a headdress, or the locks of a wig. The strings of jewels on the neck refer to a kind of collar or necklace made up of several vertical rows of decorative pearls."

[3]On the legal practices reflected in the chapter see, Meir Malul, "Adoptions of Foundlings in the Bible and Mesopotamian Documents: A Study of Some Legal Metaphors in Ezekiel 16:1-7," *Journal for the Study of the Old Testament* 46 (1990):97-126. Concerning the different metaphors used by Ezekiel in this chapter see, M. G. Swanepoel, "Ezekiel 16: Abandoned Child, Bride Adorned or Unfaithful Wife?," in *Among the Prophets: Language, Image and Structure in the Prophetic Writings*, Philip R. Davis and David J. A. Clines, eds. (Sheffield: JSOT Pres, 1993), pp.84-104.

[4]See, Joseph Blenkinsopp, *Ezekiel* (Louisville: John Knox, 1990), p. 78. For a discussion of the marriage metaphor in Ezek 16 see, July Galambush, *Jerusalem in the Book of Ezekiel: the City as Yahweh's Wife* (Atlanta, GA: Scholars, 1991), pp. 89-109. It has been rightly suggested that "the entire text [Ezek 16], however, has to be read as an allegory, and all details have to be taken as metaphors for the good deeds of YHWH for his people" (Marjo C. Annette Korpel, *A Rift in the Clouds: Ugaritic and Hebrew Descriptions of the Divine* [Munster: Ugarit-Verlag, 1990], p. 430). Cf. Swanepoel, "Ezekiel," pp. 101-103.

Jewelry was used by people belonging to the high strata of society, particularly those from the palace.[1] They dressed and adorned themselves in accordance to their social identity. This is clearly the case in Isa 3:16-26. The prophet directs his speech to the daughters of Zion, that is to say to the ladies who lived in the area of the city where the palace was located and who were rather wealthy.[2] They are proud and selfish and this is reflected in their attire and demeanor. The catalog of jewelry listed in verses 18-23 provides for us a good description of the type of jewelry used by those in high social position in Jerusalem.[3] We will say more about the significance of the jewelry mentioned in the passage, but for now we should point out that the pieces of cloth mentioned there are also indicative of social position and wealth (cf. 2 Sam 1:24), a wealth which was at least partially the result of the exploitation of the poor (cf. 3:13-15).

The "festal robes" (*ma hᵃlāsāh*) designate a costly piece of dress worn on special occasions as a symbol of high rank office (cf. Zech 3:4).[4] The Hebrew term *ma'ᵃtepet*, translated "mantle," appears to designate an "enveloping cape," an exterior garment.[5] The "cloak" was another exterior garment made of one piece of cloth worn by women (Ruth 3:15).[6] "Handbags" designates in 2 Kings 5:1, 23 a "purse" belonging to a high

---

[1]Ashurbanipal appointed officers to his court and dressed them "in multicolored garments, put golden rings in their hands, and made them do service" at his court (Oppenheim, "Babylonian," p. 296). Amen-em-heb was an Egyptian soldier under Thut-mose III whose valor was publicly recognized by Pharaoh by giving him gold in the form of "a lion, two necklaces, two flies, and four rings of finished gold" (John A Wilson, "Egyptian Historical Texts," in *Ancient Near Eastern Texts*, p. 241). In this particular case jewelry is a symbol of social status and wealth.

[2]With R. E. Clements, Isaiah 1-39 (Grand Rapids, MI: Eerdmans, 1980), p. 50. It cannot be denied that the phrase "daughters of Zion" designates in the Bible the women of Jerusalem in general (see, H. Haag, "*Bath,*" in *Theological Dictionary of the OT*, vol. 2, p. 334) but in the context of Isa 3 the main emphasis is on ladies of society; see further, Hans Wildberger, *Isaiah 1-12: A Commentary* (Minneapolis: Fortress, 1991), pp. 148-49; John D. W. Watts, *Isaiah 1-33* (Waco, TX: Word, 1985), p. 45.

[3]Elizabeth E. Platt, "Isa 3:18-23," has suggested that the jewelry and clothing mentioned in the catalog includes things worn by both women and men. She writes, "The choice of the symbols of office in jewelry, garments and cosmetics reflects the societal position of both men and women. More items belonging to men are mentioned . . ." (p. 83). See also, L. G. Running, "Garments," in *International Standard Bible Encyclopedia*, vol. 2, p. 406, who comments, "It is now being recognized that many of the terms in the Isaiah list pertain to men rather than, or as well as, to women, both as ornaments and especially as insignia of official position."

[4]Cf. Francis Brown, S. S. Driver, and Charles A. Briggs, *A Hebrew and English Lexicon of the OT* (Oxford: Clarendon, 1906), p. 323; and Ludwig Koehler, Walter Baumgartner, Johann Jakob Stamm, *The Hebrew and Arameic Lexcon of the OT* , vol 2 (Leiden: Brill, 1995), p. 569.

[5]Platt, "Isaiah 3:18-23," p. 200.

[6]Ibid., p. 80.

military officer. Term *gallāyôn*, translated "garment of gauze," is far from clear in its meaning but seems to be referring to some kind of fine or transparent cloth.[1] It is impossible to be certain of its real meaning. The same is true about the word *sadîn*, "linen garments." It seemed to have been a very valuable article of clothing.[2] The "turban" was a headgear made of a piece of fine clothe wrapped around the head and worn by the high priest (Exod 29:6; Zech 3:5) and by kings (Isa 62:3).[3] The last piece of clothing, "veils," could be designating an outer garment embroidered with metallic threads.[4] The text suggests that this kind of clothing was a sign of social status and, therefore, available to persons of financial resources. Together with jewelry they were symbols of the person's position in society.

The dress and jewelry of the high priest were also an expression of his position in society. The text states that one of their purposes was "for glory" (*lᵉkābôd*, Exod 28:2), an expression which addresses the social "weight" or importance of the high priest in Israel, the prestige he enjoyed among his people.[5] "Glory" (*kābôd*) describes "what adds to a person's standing, what increases a person's position and influence"[6] and serves in the present passage to describe the role of the high priest in Israel as the maximum religious leader.

5. Symbol of Power/Authority

A high office in society is usually accompanied by power and authority. Jewelry could express both ideas. For instance the royal crown is a symbol of status and power to rule over others (2 Kings 11:12; Esther 8:15; Zech 6:11-13);[7] removing the crown from the head of a king means to be humiliated, to lose power (2 Sam 12:30; Jer 13:18; Ezek 21:26 [31]). The

---

[1]Cf. Wildberger, *Isaiah 1-12*, p. 155.

[2]Ibid. Platt has suggested that it designates a warrior's belt. This is possible but not absolutely certain ("Isaiah 3:18-23," p. 79).

[3]Wildberger, *Isaiah 1-12*, ibid., p. 155; and Platt, "Isaiah 3:18-23," pp. 78-79.

[4]Platt, Ibid., p. 80.

[5]Claus Westermann, "*Kbd* schwer sein," in *THAT* 1:799-800.

[6]Georg Molin, "Glory," in *Encyclopedia of Biblical Theology*, Johannes B. Bauer, ed. (New York: Crossroad, 1981), p. 295.

[7]See, L. E. Toombs, "Crown," in *Interpreter's Dictionary of the Bible*, vol. 1, p. 746.

seal was also a symbol of power and authority.[1] Seals were made of different materials including semi-precious stones and gold and were usually "beyond the means of the common man."[2]

The legal significance of seals made them a natural symbol of power and authority (cf. Gen 38:18, 25). This is particularly the case with the sealing ring that a king gives to his prime minister. Pharaoh deputized power to Joseph by giving him his ring and a gold chain (Gen 41:42). Xerxes gave his signet ring to Haman granting him power to legislate (Esther 3:10, 12); later he withdrew that power from him, took the ring and gave it to Mordecai empowering him to legally protect his people (8:2, 8,10). Clearly the seal was in those cases a symbol of deputized power (cf. Isa 3:21).[3]

6. Religious Function

One of the basic purposes of jewelry was religious, consisting in the manifestation of the religious convictions and/or function of the person wearing it. Several examples from the OT illustrate this usage. The first one is the jewelry of the high priest.[4] We have already indicated that it expressed beauty and social status but it also communicated profound religious

---

[1]For the ancient Near Eastern background consult, Leonard Gorelick and A. John Gwinnett, "The Ancient Near Eastern Cylinder Seal as Social Emblem and Status Symbol," *Journal of Near Eastern Studies* 49 (1990):45-56.

[2]William W. Hallo, "'As the Seal upon Thine Arm': Glyptic Metaphors in the Biblical World," in *Ancient Seals and the Bible*, Leonard Gorelick and Elizabeth Williams-Forte, eds (California: Undena Publications, 1983), p. 8. See also, L. G. Herr, "Seal," in *International Standard Bible Encyclopedia*, vol. 4, p. 371. In one of Sargon's letters to Assur during his eighth campaign he describes a seal he took from a temple: "1 seal ring of gold (used) to validating (lit. completing) the decrees of Bagbartu, the spouse of Haldia, was completely covered (full) with precious stones" (Luckenbill, *Ancient Records*, vol. 2, p. 97).

[3]Herr, "Seal," p. 370.

[4]In the ancient Near East the style of the priestly dress may have varied from country to country. We know that in Assyria sometimes the priests officiated naked in rituals that required cultic nudity (H. W. F. Saggs, *The Mighty that Was Assyria* [London: Sidgwick and Jackson, 1984], p. 152). This was also the case among the Sumerians (Helmer Ringgren, "*Kohen* Ancient Near East: Mesopotamia," *Theological Dictionary of the OT*, vol. 7, p. 63). Among the Akkadian the priests wore linen garments of different colors (ibid., p. 64). In Egypt the Pharaoh was the only one who could approach the gods and the priests functioned as his representatives. It is probable that the high priest may have been dressed like a king. The priests wore special clothes which in some cases were richly decorated and adorned with jewelry (Herman T. Velde, "Theology. Priests, and Worship in Ancient Egypt," in *Civilizations of the Ancient Near East*, vol. 3, Jack M. Sasson, ed. [New York: Macmillan, 1995], pp. 1732-33). Among the Hittites temple personnel were not allowed to wear jewelry of gold, silver, or bronze. If any of those metals were given to them they were not to make ornaments for their wives and children but were rather expected to sell them in court. This was done to protect the gold, silver and bronze that belonged to the temple (Cord Kuhne, "Hittite Texts: Instructions for Cultic Officials and Temple Personnel," in *Near Eastern Religious Texts Relating to the OT*, Walter Beyerlin, ed. [Philadelphia: Westminster, 1978], pp. 182-83).

convictions. In fact it identified him as a religious leader not a military or civil one. A golden plate was attached to the crown of the high priest with an engraved inscription on it: "Holy to the Lord" (Exod 28:36-38), which identified the nature of his work. It was related to his work as an instrument in the atonement process (vs. 38). One of the Hebrew words used to refer to the crown is *nezer*, which is the noun form of verb *nzr*, "to consecrate" (29:6; cf. Zech 6:11). The noun identifies the crown as a sign of the consecration of the high priest to the Lord.[1]

The two onyx stones on the shoulder pieces of the ephod with the names of the twelve tribes engraved on them (28:9-14) and the twelve semi-precious stones on the breast piece of the priestly dress (28:17-30)[2] had also a religious motivation. They served as a remembrance before the Lord (vss. 12, 29). In his person the high priest took the Israelites before the Lord as their representative. One could say that the stones reminded him of his function but at the same time they were "an invocation to God to be mindful of His people Israel, with whom He enacted a covenant."[3]

The priestly robe had at its hem tassels of pomegranate of three colors with bells of gold between them (28:31-35). Pomegranates were fruits of the land of Israel and seemed to have been "symbols of beauty and of the fruitfulness of Yahweh's provisions"[4] (Num 13:23; Deut 8:8;

---

[1]J. Kuhlewein, "*Nazir*," in *THAT* 2:51.

[2]It is very difficult to identify the stones mentioned in the Hebrew text. For a good attempt see, J. S. Harris, "The Stones of the High Priest's Breastplate," *Annual of the Leeds University Oriental Society* 5 (1963-65):40-62.

[3]Sarna, *Exodus*, p. 179. The semi-precious stones on the shoulder and breastplate of the high priest looked like seals, i.e. stones on which a name, the name of the owner, was engraved (this was also noticed by Platt, "Jewelry," p. 830). This underscores the functional nature of the stones. A seal was an extension of the presence, authority and power of the individual and represented him or her. This use of semi-precious stones contrast very markedly with the significance of semi-precious and precious stones in the ancient Near East where they were associated with different deities and considered to posses prophylactic and therapeutic qualities; see E. A. Wallis Budge, *Amulets and Superstitions* (New York, NY: Dover, 1930), pp. 306-325. Their use as ornaments was probably secondary, being their primary function religious and magical. For instance, in Egypt turquoise was associated with the goddess Hathor, called "the Lady of Turquoise" ("Turquoise," in Ian Shaw and Paul Nicholson, *British Museum Dictionary of Ancient Egypt* [Cairo, Egypt: American University in Cairo Press, 1995], p. 297). The magical effects of those stones were well known and their use important because "the wearer was afforded protection from unknown hostile forces, such as diseases and noxious animals, by talismans made of carnelian, turquoise, lapis lazuli, and artificial fabrications that were tied to the neck, waist, wrists, and anklets" (R. G. Bullard, "Stones, Precious," *International Standard Bible Encyclopedia*, vol. 4, p. 624).

[4]Durham, *Exodus*, p. 388; cf. Sarna, *Exodus*, p. 182.

Song 4:3, 13; 6:7, 11; 7:13; 8:2). The function of the bells is not clear but they may have had the purpose of assuring those outside the holy place that the high priest had not died during the performance of his ministry before the Lord.[1]

It is obvious that the main function of the jewelry worn by the high priest was religious and that it was directly and exclusively related to his work. This explains the absence of similar jewelry on the vestment of other priests. Jewelry was not prescribed by the Lord to anybody else in Israel. Perhaps the only exception may have been the crown of the king of Israel which was somewhat similar to the priestly one. It also signaled the fact that the king was anointed and consecrated by the Lord to his office (2 Kings 11:12).[2]

Nevertheless, some Israelites did wear religious jewelry. Reference to this type of jewelry is found in Isa 3:16-21. The terminology used to designate the different pieces of jewelry has been difficult to understand and in some cases practically impossible, but archaeology and the study of ancient Near Eastern iconography has shed some light on a number of them.[3]

A number of jewelry items are clearly associated with religious ideas. The "anklets" are ankle-bangles associated with fertility figurines in the surrounding cultures[4] and express the religious beliefs of the wearer. It is now known that the "headbands" designate pendants on a necklace representing the sun god and that the Hebrew term could be translated "sun/star disk." The "crescents" were ornaments in the form of the moon (cf. Judg 8:21, 26), representing

---

[1]Kaiser, "Exodus," p. 467.

[2]Toombs, "Crown," p. 746.

[3]See, Platt, "Isa 3:18-23," p. 71-78, 194-99; *idem.*, "Jewelry," pp. 830-32; and Wildberger, *Isaiah 1-12*, pp. 148-54.

[4]The description of the different type of jewelry in Isa 3 is indebted to Platt, "Jewelry," pp. 831-32. Since I will only deal with some of the items, I would like to provide for the reader the full list, as translated in the RSV, with Platt's suggestions in parenthesis: (1) anklets (ankle bangles), (2) headbands (sun- or star-disks), (3) crescents (crescents), (4) pendants (drop pendants), (5) bracelets (necklace cords), (6) scarfs (beads), (7) headdresses (garland crowns), (8) armlets (armlets or foot jewelry), (9) sashes (sashes or girdles), (10) perfume boxes (tubular "soul" cases), (11) amulets (snake charms), (12) signet rings (signet rings), (13) nose rings (nose rings), (14) festal robes (loin clothes), (15) mantles (enveloping capes), (16) cloaks (mantles), (17) handbags (wallets), (18) garments of gauze (thin garments), (19) linen garments (warriors' belts), (20) turbans (turbans), and (21) veils (outer cloaks).

a deity.[1] The "pendants" were probably bead-like pendants, made of semiprecious stones or other materials, placed on necklaces together with the crescents.

This type of jewelry is associated in the OT with idolatry. This explains in part why the Lord will remove (*sûr*) them from the people. The verb *sûr* "is used elsewhere to speak of the removal of idols (Gen 35:2; Josh 24:14, 23 . . .). A direct connection is drawn here between such luxury in ornament and dress and idolatry."[2] The same phenomenon is described in Hosea 2:13 (15) in association with the worship of Baal.[3]

7. Magical/Apotropaic Function

Closely related to the religious use, and probably inseparable from it, was the use of jewelry to protect the individual from evil powers and dangers.[4] This usage was well known throughout the ancient Near East but is not explicitly found in the OT. Evidence of its presence is provided in Isa 3:20. The phrase "perfume boxes" is a common translation of the Hebrew *bāttê hannepheš* (lit. "soul houses"), now recognized to be a wrong translation. Although the exact meaning of the phrase is not certain it is now generally accepted that it refers to some kind of amulet.[5] The same phrase has been found in Jewish Aramaic inscriptions to designate a

---

[1]Wildberger, *Isaiah 1-12*, p. 152, has suggested that the women of Zion who wore the sun and moon pendants "would probably not even have known that these articles of jewelry were originally symbols of the sun and moon deity and, as such, had a religious meaning (as amulets or as a guarantee of fertility)." This is difficult to accept because it implies ignorance of the religious practices of the surrounding cultures on the part of the Israelite society. Isaiah indicates that part of the problem of the leaders of Israel and of the people in general was precisely the worship of pagan deities. Crescents and suns or five-pointed stars were also considered to be "prophylactic signs against the Evil Eye" (Yedida Kalfon Stillman, *Palestinian Costume and Jewelry*, [Albuquerque, NM: University of New Mexico Press, 1979], p. 97). On the symbolism of the sun and moon pendants see, Maxwell-Hyslop, *Jewelry*, pp. 140-51. Soldiers wore jewelry with those designs "to show that the gods were accompanying the Babylonian and Assyrian rulers on their campaigns . . ." (Ibid., p. 152).

[2]John D. W. Watts, *Isaiah 1-33* (Waco, TX: Word, 1985), p. 45.

[3]See, Douglas Stuart, *Hoseah-Jonah* (Waco, TX: Word, 1987), p. 52; cf. Francis I. Andersen and David Noel Freedman, *Hosea* (New York: Doubleday, 1980), pp. 259-62.

[4]Healing power was assigned to a necklace of semi-precious stones (R. Caplice, "Namburbi Texts in the British Museum-1," *Orientalia* 34 [1965]:129), and one of amber beads protected from evil eye (Stillman, p. 94). In fact, as pointed out above, precious metals and stones were believed to have magical powers (Maxwell-Hyslop, *Jewelry*, pp. lxiii-lxiv). On the Evil Eye consult, Marie-Louise Thomsen, "The Evil Eye in Mesopotamia," *Journal of Near Eastern Studies* 51 (1992):19-32.

[5]Wildberger, *Isaiah*, p. 153; and Platt, "Jewelry," p. 832.

funerary monument.[1] This suggests that we may be dealing here with a type of amulet related to the cult of the dead that could protect its wearer from evil or be a source of blessings.[2] It could very well have been a tubular case with some written text in it.[3]

Another term for jewelry in Isaiah that suggests a magical or apotropaic usage is the "amulets" (vs 20). The Hebrew term *lehaš* contains the idea of "conjuring" and "charming" (Isa 3:3). It is generally recognized that the term designates an amulet that protected perhaps from snakes ("snake charms")[4] and which was put on a necklace or on a wrist chain.[5] The presence of religious and magic jewelry in the catalog of Isa 3 indicates that the pride of the "daughters of Zion" was not just based on their financial security, their beauty, or their social position, but specially on the psychological security that religious and magical pieces of jewelry provided for them. It is this type of pride that became the main target of the prophetic speech. The presence of religious and magical jewelry also suggests that the prophet is not simply attacking its use as a sign of haughtiness and ostentation[6] but that he is in fact condemning the jewelry he is listing. Otherwise he would be saying that wearing pagan religious,

---

[1]Charles-F. Jean and Jacob Hoftijzer, *Dictionnaire des inscriptions sémitiques de l'ouest* (Leiden: Brill, 1965), pp. 35, 185.

[2]The cult of the dead was widespread in the ancient world and was practiced by some Israelites as part of their "popular religion." On this subject consult, Theodore J. Lewis, *Cults of the Dead in Ancient Israel and Ugarit* (Atlanta, GA: Scholars, 1989); *idem.*, "Ancestor Worship," *Anchor Bible Dictionary*, vol. 1, pp. 240-42; and Charles A. Kennedy, "Dead, Cult of the," Ibid., vol. 2, pp. 105-8. There might be a possible connection between the use of the phrase "soul houses" of Isaiah and the Egyptian "soul houses" located by the entrance of the shaft-burials of relatively poor people. These "soul houses" are considered to be "elaborate forms of offering tables. Flinders Petrie, . . . was able to trace the evolution of soul houses from simple pottery trays (imitating stone offering tables) to later more elaborate examples consisting of models of houses, the forecourt of which were strewn with food offerings" (Ian Shaw and Paul Nicholson, *British Museum Dictionary of Ancient Egypt* [Cairo, Egypt: American University in Cairo Press, 1995], p. 209).

[3]As suggested by Platt, "Isa 3:18-23," pp. 198-99.

[4]Ibid., p. 77.

[5]Amulets were often carried under the garments. In an oracle Ninlil said to Ashurbanipal, "I have placed you like an *amulet* on my breast. At night I place spread over you all day I keep a cover on you" (Robert H. Pfeiffer, "Oracle of Ninlil Concerning Ashurbanipal," in *ANET*, p. 451). Cf. Songs 8:6; and William W. Hallo, "For Love is Strong as Death," *Journal of Ancient Near Eastern Society of Columbia University* 22 (1993):45-50. Concerning the symbolism of amulets see, E. Douglas Van Buren, "Amulets in Ancient Mesopotamia," *Orientalia* 14 (1954):18-23; *idem.*, "Amulets, Symbols or Idols?" *Iraq* 12 (1950):193-96. On Hebrew amulets, Ada Yardeni, "Remarks on the Priestly Blessing and Two Ancient Amulets from Jerusalem," *Vetus Testamentum* 41 (1991):176-85.

[6]That is what Horsnell, *"dh,"* *New International Dictionary of OT Theology and Exegesis*, vol. 3, p. 322, 323, suggests.

magical and superstitious jewelry was acceptable as long as it was not extravagant and a sign of pride.

8. *Used as Offerings*

Jewelry was used as offerings for the gods.[1] In fact, in some cases a specific item of jewelry was made and given to the temple to be placed on the image of the god. Such a practice is foreign to the OT but we do find the idea of giving jewelry as an offering to the Lord. This was done specially after a census was taken (Num 31:50; cf. Exod 30:11-16) and was associated with the idea of atonement. This jewelry belonged to the temple treasury and may have been used to make or replace vessels of gold or simply as a kind of memorial.

C. Old Testament Attitude Toward Jewelry

Our previous discussion has shown that the Israelites used jewelry for the same reasons and purposes that it was used throughout the ancient Near East. The Old Testament materials indicate that the use of jewelry among the Israelites did not necessarily reflect the attitude of the biblical Israelite religion toward jewelry. It is this fine distinction that we now want to explore. Although the Old Testament does not completely reject the use of jewelry, it is interesting to observe that there is only one incident in which jewelry is officially prescribed to someone, specifically to the high priest. There are several things that we should observe about this case. First, the jewelry he wore was beautiful but simple in its design. The semi precious stones were engraved with the names of the tribes and the frontlet of gold had an inscription on it. Second, the pieces of jewelry belonged to the priestly vestment and therefore were to be worn whenever he officiated as high priest. He was authorized to wear a type of jewelry that made a clear statement concerning his distinctive function within the Yahwistic faith and its cultus. Third, not one item of the priestly jewelry was placed directly on his body but rather on his garment. Removal of his garment was a removal of jewelry. This may seem to be an insignificant detail but we should remember that wearing jewelry may have required damaging the

---

[1]See, Maxwell-Hyslop, *Jewelry*, p. 132. Ashurbanipal wrote, "I made (the images of) their great godheads sumptuous with red gold and shining stones. I presented them with golden jewelry and many other precious objects which I had won as booty" (Oppenheim, "Babylonian," p.559). A devotee of Inanna gave her a treasure of precious stones and ornaments which she used to bedeck the different parts of her body (S. N. Kramer, "Love in the Gipar," in *ANET*, p. 638).

body, e.g, perforating the ears and the nose, which would have been rejected by the Yahwistic faith.[1] Fourth, jewelry was prescribed here exclusively for the high priest and not for the Israelites in general. The OT does not prescribe any religious jewelry for the Israelites to use in order to indicate that they worshiped Yahweh. An Israelite was to be identified as such by placing tassels to the hem of their garments with a blue cord attached to them (Num 15:37-41).[2] In fact, what distinguished them above anything else as worshippers of Yahweh was their obedient commitment to the Lord, their holy lives. It was to this fact that the tassels with their blue cord pointed (15:39-40).

The functional use of jewelry to indicate royal status was commonly accepted in the OT, although there is no clear, official prescription for it. Sometimes when the prophets wanted to identify a person as a king, queen, or prince they described their vestments and jewelry because these revealed the status they had achieved. One could also include here the seal whose purpose was not primarily ornamental but functional. The use of jewelry as currency and as evidence of wealth is not condemned, obviously because of functional and pragmatic reasons. But apart from these cases the OT seems to have a pejorative attitude toward the significance of jewelry. This is indicated in several ways.

First, there is a tendency in the OT to devalue the significance of jewelry as a symbol of financial security. This is quite common in the wisdom literature where wisdom and a good wife are considered more precious than jewels (Prov 3:15; Job 28:15-19; Prov 31:10). If one were to choose between instruction and silver and gold, instruction should take precedence (Prov 8:10; 11:22). The "lips of knowledge" are considered to be "a precious jewel" (20:15). This is not an open condemnation of jewelry but a devaluation of it as a symbol of ultimate value.

Second, the OT rejects the religious and magical usages of jewelry by the people and associates them directly with idolatry. When Jacob was returning to Bethel the Lord commanded him and those with him to remove their gods and to consecrate themselves to Him (Gen 35:4). As a response they gave Jacob all

---

[1]According to W. L. Reed, "physical mutilation of the bodies of man and beasts was not common in biblical times, because of the belief in the sacredness of life" ("Mutilation," in *Interpreter's Dictionary of the Bible*, vol. 3, p. 477). It has been suggested that "the Law forbade all mutilation of the body and so they [Israelite women] could not pierce their nose or ears to hold the ornaments" (Henri Daniel-Rops, *Daily Life in the Time of Jesus* [New York: Hawthorn, 1962], p. 250). Yet, we know that in some cases earrings had a pin long enough to pass over the whole ear (Maxwell-Hyslop, *Jewelry*, p. 5).

[2]For an analysis of this practice see, Jacob Milgrom, "Of Hems and Tassels," *Biblical Archaeology Review* 9 (1983):61-65.

the foreign gods they had in their hands and the earrings. These were obviously "ornaments that carried some kind of religious significance, possibly with iconic impressions on them."[1] The implication is that this type of jewelry was incompatible with the worship of Yahweh. Jacob hid them under a tree.[2]

In Exodus 33:4-6 we find another incident in which God commanded the Israelites to remove their jewelry. This happened immediately after the worship of the golden calf when God was angered at them. Among other things God ordered them to remove their ornaments. Scholars have taken the removal of jewelry to be a sign of mourning, which is compatible with ancient Near Eastern practices,[3] and "as a test of their repentance."[4] Others have argued that this "was not a sign of mourning but compliance with God's command to Moses (vs. 5)."[5] There is also the possibility that the request "may be based upon the fact that they were wearing jewelry associated with foreign Gods."[6] Undoubtedly, the removal of jewelry is associated here with several ideas. Among them we find idolatry, God's reaction to that sin, and a spirit of repentance. The immediate context puts the emphasis on the people's spirit of remorse as they humbled themselves before the Lord. This is similar to what we found in the case of Jacob. However, there is something new in this narrative in that the passage ends with a kind of enigmatic phrase: "The people of Israel stripped themselves of their ornaments, *from Mount Horeb onward*."[7] This suggests that the

---

[1]Hamilton, *Genesis 18-50*, p. 375 n. 15. Westermann considers the earrings to be amulets (*Genesis 12-36*, p. 551; cf. Sarna, *Genesis*, p. 240).

[2]There has been some discussion on the significance of this act; see, Eduard Nielsen, "The Burial of the Foreign Gods," *Studia Theologica* 8 (1954-55):103-22, and commentaries.

[3]E.g. Childs, *Exodus*, p. 589. Adad-guppi, the mother of Nabonidus, wrote, "In order to appease (the anger of) my personal god and goddess, I did not permit apparel made of fine wool, gold and silver jewelry, any new garment, perfumes, and scented oil to touch my body, I was clad in a torn garment and when I left (my house) it was in silence, I constantly pronounced benedictions for them . . ." (Oppenheim, "Babylonian," p. 560). The parallel with the biblical story is very limited and the purpose seems to be significantly different.

[4]Kaiser, "Exodus," p. 482-83.

[5]J. Coert Rylaarsdam, "The Book of Exodus," *Interpreter's Bible*, vol. 1, George A. Buttrick. (Nashville, TN: Abingdon, 1952), p. 1071.

[6]Hyatt, *Exodus*, p. 14.

[7]The phrase *mē har Hôrē b* should not be rendered "at Mount Horeb" (NIV), because it would require the use of the preposition *bᵉ* instead of *min*. The preposition min has a temporal significance here and can be translated "*from* Mount Horeb on." On this use of the preposition see Bruce K. Waltke and M. O'Connor, *An Introduction to Biblical Hebrew Syntax* (Winona Lake, IN: Eisenbraun, 1990), pp. 212-13.

removal of jewelry as a sign of repentance or mourning "was not a temporary display, but a continuous one."[1] It became "a perpetual rule,"[2] a constant manifestation of the Israelites' dependence and reliance on God's forgiving grace.

It is indeed difficult to know for how long the Israelites did not wear jewelry. It has been suggested that this was the case only during the wilderness wanderings but this is just a conjecture.[3] Judges 8:24 seems to suggest that during the period of the judges "ornaments were not worn" by the Israelites.[4] We recognize that it is difficult to prove a direct connection between the incident on Mount Horeb and this one in the period of the judges but the canonical form of the text allows for a possible connection. We do know that the Israelites did wear jewelry but it may not have been that common. The archaeological evidence suggests that jewelry was not habitual among the Israelites and what has been found is usually of inferior quality.[5] It has been indicated that "Israel, in many respects, must have seemed a nation of puritans in the ancient world, not only in worship and morals, but even in dress."[6] This could have been the case in early Israel, but by the time of Hosea (2:13 [15]) and Isaiah (3:16-23) religious and ornamental jewelry was very popular among the Israelites.

Isaiah's attack on jewelry, which we have mentioned several times, was a condemnation of jewelry as a religious and social symbol and as an expression of pride.[7] Undoubtedly, this was a common condition among those in high positions in the palace. Hans Wildberger perceptively argues that the catalogue of jewelry in Isa 3 "betrays the influence that the palace had on the lifestyle of the

---

[1]Childs, *Exodus*, p. 589, who adds, "Although the terminology of repentance is not used, the tradition of the stripping of ornaments—whatever it may have once meant—now serves in the narrative to demonstrate Israel's change of heart."

[2]Cole, *Exodus*, pp. 222-23.

[3]Sarna, *Exodus*, p. 211.

[4]George F. Moore, *Critical and Exegetical Commentary on Judges* (Edinburgh: T. & T. Clark, 1895), p. 23; and Cole, *Exodus*, p. 213.

[5]See, Platt, "Jewelry," p. 827; Rosenthal, *Jewelry*, p. 54; and Avraham Negev, ed., *The Archaeological Encyclopedia of the Holy Land* [Nashville, TN: Thomas Nelson, 1986], p. 203). P. L. Garber and R. W. Funk, "Jewels and Precious Stones," *Interpreter's Dictionary of the Bible*, vol. 2, p. 899, where he states, "It would appear that in contrast to the many kinds of jewels that were known, the early Israelites actually must have possessed small quantities of jewels, precious stones, or decorative minerals. In Palestinian excavations . . . comparatively slight evidence for precious stones have been found."

[6]Cole, *Exodus*, pp. 222-23.

[7]It is sometimes argued that the prophet's attack is not against wearing jewelry and beautiful apparel but that "the lesson is on the misuse of the authority of office for which that apparel stands" (Platt, "Isa 3:18-23," p. 200). But this overlooks the pagan ideas associated and expressed through the dress style used by those leaders and against which the prophet had already reacted (2:8, 18, 20). It is probably this same kind of apparel that Zephaniah condemns in 2:8.

leading citizens of the capital city. Without intending to do so, it indicates how intensely Israel allowed itself to be influenced by foreign custom."[1]

Third, there is some indirect evidence that seems to indicate that Yahwistic faith was not positively predisposed toward jewelry. It is interesting to notice that precious stones and metals are not directly associated with the creation of Adam and Eve. This is an argument from silence; yet some of those metals and stones are mentioned in the creation account in Gen 2:11,12 and we are informed that they were located outside the garden of Eden, in the land of Havilah. This is surprising if we take into consideration that in ancient Near Eastern mythology the garden of the gods were embellished with precious stones.[2]

What is important for our purpose is that in the creation of Adam and Eve jewelry played no role at all and that no reference to it was made when the Lord provided clothes for them and dressed them (Gen 3:21). They were both created in God's image and it was this fact that allowed them to rule over the rest of the created world. It would appear that there is here an implicit devaluation of the use of jewelry for personal adornment and to define or represent one's social status or power and authority. Adam and Eve functioned as rulers of God's creation because they bore in their own person and character the *image* of God.

It is also important to observe that Yahweh is never described in the OT as wearing jewelry. This is again surprising because in the ancient Near East the gods were bedecked with jewelry.[3] One of the reasons for this could be that since there is no

---

[1] *Isaiah*, p. 155.

[2] We read in the "Epic of Gilgamesh," ix.v 47-vi.35, "Before him there were trees of precious stones, and he went straight to look at them. The trees bears carnelian as its fruit, laden with clusters (of jewels), dazzling to behold,–it bears lapis lazuli as foliage, bearing fruit, a delight to look upon" (Maureen Gallery Kovacs, *The Epic of Gilgamesh: Translated, with Introduction* [Stanford, CA: University Press, 1985], pp. 78-78); among the stones mentioned in the rest of the broken text describing the garden we find agate, jasper, rubies, hematite, and emeralds. See also, Howard N. Wallace, *The Eden Narrative* (Atlanta, GA: Scholars, 1985), pp. 71-72; U. Cassuto, *A Commentary on the Book of Genesis*, vol. 1 (Jerusalem: Magness Press, 1961), pp. 77-79.

[3] An example from Egypt is found in the Stela of Ikhernofret, from the time of Sesostris III (1874-1855 BC). The priest was responsible to organize the annual festival of the Mysteries of Osiris during which, he says, "I decked the breast of the lord of Abydos with lapis lazuli and turquoise, fine gold, and all costly stones which are the ornaments of a god's body" (Miriam Lichtheim, *Ancient Egyptian Literature: A Book of Readings-Volume I: The Old and Middle Kingdoms* [Los Angeles, CA: University of California Press, 1973], p. 124). Nebuchadnezzar prepared for the gods Ea and Nebo "[a fabric befitting a] god [. . . embroidered] and made sparkling with precious stones and gold (-appliqués) was its front. I had made [lit. fit] beautifully into garments befitting their godheads . . ." (Oppenheim, "Babylonian," p.310). This type of dress probably represented the kind of dress worn by the king himself. In the myth of the descent of Inanna to the underworld we find a list of the jewelry she wore (S. N. Kramer, "Inanna's Descent to the Nether World," in *ANET*, p. 53). This text was the prototype for the myth of the descent of Ishtar which also contains a list of the jewelry she wore; for the text and its translation see, W. F. Leemans, *Ishtar of Lagaba and Her Dress* (Leiden: Brill, 1952). Maxwell-Hyslop, *Jewelry*, p. 133, comments concerning that text, "We know that these ornaments were not only used by goddesses, but formed part of the normal collection for jewellery worn by women of high rank." Canaanite gods and goddesses wore jewelry to enhance their beauty and power (Korpel, *Rift in the Clouds*, p. 427).

image of Him it is not possible to embellish Him through jewelry. But at a deeper level we have to take into consideration that He created all precious stones and metals and that they cannot contribute to His own beautification.

Why then did God create precious metals and stones? Possibly to adorn or beautify the world. In Gen 2:11,12 they are located in a place where there are no human beings, a place untouched by human hand, embellishing the land of Havilah. This may sound like unfounded speculation if it were not for the fact that in other places in the OT precious metals and stones embellish the place were God stands (Exod 24:10) and dwells (26:26; 29) and will be used to adorn the place where His people will dwell (Isa 54:11,12; cf. Rev 21:15-21).

D. Conclusion

One could conclude that the OT has a restrictive attitude toward the use of jewelry. We have seen that its beauty and value are recognized. What makes it impossible to conclude that Israel's official faith absolutely rejected the use of jewelry is the fact that God commanded that the high priest be adorned with it in order to signal his religious function. In addition one could detect a "tolerance" of the use of jewelry as a symbol of social status and authority. This is particularly the case with the king and the queen and with the use of seals.

It is interesting to observe that although the high priest was authorized to wear jewelry as a religious symbol, there is no authorization allowing the Israelites to do the same. This was indeed strange in a world in which individuals wore jewelry to express their religious convictions and to demonstrate their commitment to a particular god or gods. Israelites were to express their religious convictions and commitment to Yahweh through a holy life and not through external adornment. It appears that the OT does reject the use of religious jewelry by the Israelites. In addition, the magic use of jewelry is clearly rejected since in the ancient Near East it is inseparable from the religious usage and from idolatry.

God's command to the Israelites to remove their jewelry permanently at Sinai is intriguing. The command was to remove all of it, implying that it was not to be used for adornment, as a symbol of authority, or as designating social status or religious convictions. Here we have an indication of God's intentions for His people. They were ordered to remove them from their persons but not to get rid of them. The implications is that jewelry retained its function as currency and personal wealth, which was to be put at the service of the Lord.

Reasons for the OT restrictive attitude toward jewelry could be found in the fact that it is associated with idolatry and at times with the abuse and exploitation of the poor. But the issue goes deeper than that. Jewelry seems to be generally perceived as the embodiment of human pride and self-reliance, both closely related to idolatry. A change in the heart of the individual from hubris to submissiveness to Yahweh was indicated through the removal of jewelry, the absence of which became a reminder of God's forgiving grace. Perhaps, this was based on biblical anthropology which conceived of the person as an integral unit in whom the exterior and the inner personal convictions were practically inseparable. What an Israelite was expressed itself in what she or he did, said, and to some extent, wore.

JEWELRY IN THE NT:
A DESCRIPTION OF ITS FUNCTION

A. Introduction

New Testament passages on jewelry are not as abundant as in the Old Testament but the few we find can be grouped according to the function and purpose of jewelry. These functions are basically the same we found in the Old Testament with the exception of references to religious or protective jewelry. Some of the passages are brief and clear while others are more difficult to interpret. Part of the problem is that the terminology for jewelry in the New Testament is almost limited to terms such as "gold," "silver" and "pearls." In some cases we are not certain whether those terms are being used to designate pieces of jewelry. There are very few references to precious stones used for personal adornment. Because of their importance to our subject, two key passages deserve a detailed exegesis of their content, namely 1 Pet 3:1-6 and 1 Tim 2:8-10. But first we should explore the different purposes of jewelry in the New Testament and their significance.

A. Uses of Jewelry in the New Testament
1. Used as Adornment

The use of jewelry as adornment was well known during the period of the New Testament. Peter and Paul refer to it and mention gold and pearls used by women to beautify themselves (1 Pet 3:3; 1 Tim 2:9).[1] Peter describes this adornment as exterior in contrast to the true adornment which is interior and expresses itself in a gentle and quiet spirit (1 Pet 3:4). For Paul the adornment of a Christian consists of good deeds (1 Tim 2:10). (For a discussion of those two passages see the next two chapters).

Clear reference to the use of jewelry as personal adornment is also found in the description of Babylon, the apocalyptic prostitute. She is depicted as a queen, "dressed in purple and scarlet, and was glittering with gold, precious stones and pearls" (Rev 17:4; cf. 18:16).[2] In this particular case

---

[1]G. Schneider, *"Chrysos Gold," Exegetical Dictionary of the NT*, vol. 3, edited by Horst Balz and Gerhard Schneider (Grand Rapids, MI: Eerdmans, 1993), p. 490. The Greek term *chrysos* is rendered "gold ornaments" in 1 Tim 2:9 by Walter Bauer, William F. Arndt and F. Wilbur Gingrich, *A Greek Lexicon of the NT and Other Early Christian Literature* (Cambridge: University Press, 1957), p. 897.

[2]"The woman was royally robed; *purple and scarlet* were colors of splendour and magnificence. They were not for the poor since the dyes producing them were very expensive" (Leon Morris, *Revelation* [Grand Rapids, MI: Eerdmans, 1987], p. 199; cf. G. B. Caird, *A Commentary on the Revelation of John the Divine* [New York, NY: Harper and Row, 1966], p. 213).

"gold" designates "gold ornaments."[1] In some ways the description of this woman is similar to that of Israel in Ezekiel 16. The nation is portrayed as a queen, richly dressed and adorned, who rejected the Lord and prostituted herself with the kings of the earth. They were to destroy her and remove the jewelry from her (16:39,40). In Revelation the apocalyptic prostitute will be hated by the kings of the earth who "will bring her to ruin and leave her naked; they will eat her flesh and burn her with fire" (17:16).

One can hardly overlook the fact that another woman is mentioned in Revelation but her adornment is essentially different from the one worn by the prostitute. This time the woman represents the people of God. She has a crown consisting of twelve stars (12:1) and is dressed with the sun and not, like her counterpart, with fine linen glittering with gold and with precious stones. One should also notice the impressive contrast between the dress and adornment of the prostitute and the white "robes of the heavenly multitudes of the returning Lord (19:14) and of the members of the salvation community who have remained faithful (3:18; 6:11; 7:9)."[2] White is the color of heavenly glory and seems to be symbolic of purity, obedience, glory, and victory.[3]

The beauty of jewels is recognized in the book of Revelation and is used to describe and symbolize the tremendous and inexpressible beauty of the New Jerusalem (21:11). The wall and foundations of the city are described as made of different precious stones and its street and buildings of gold (21:18-21). The city is described as a queen who is getting married and using nuptial imagery she is depicted as "a bride beautifully dressed for her husband" (21:2).[4] The use of gold, silver and costly stones in the

---

[1]Bauer, *Lexicon*, p. 897.

[2]Jürgen Roloff, *Revelation: A Continental Commentary* (Minneapolis, MN: Fortress, 1993), p. 197. Philip Edgcumbe Hughes contrasts the display of adornment of the prostitute woman in Rev 17:4 with the advice given by Paul and Peter to Christian women in 1 Tim 2:9,10 and 1 Pet 3:3,4 (*The Book of Revelation* [Grand Rapids, MI: Eerdmans, 1990], pp. 182-183).

[3]Roloff, *Revelation*, p. 197 and J.-A. Bühner, "*Leukos* white, radiant," *Exegetical Dictionary of the NT*, vol. 2, p. 350.

[4]For a discussion on the background of the nuptial imagery used in Rev 19-21 see, Jan Fekkes III, "'His Bride Has Prepared Herself': Revelation 19-21 and Isaian Nuptial Imagery," *Journal of Biblical Literature* 109 (1990):269-87. Concerning the adornments he writes, "The glorious bridal attire and ornaments of the New Jerusalem reach back from the future into the present and serve as a symbolic testimony to the faithfulness of the earthly community. Just as the fine linen of the bride stands as a metaphor for the 'righteous deeds of the saints' (19:8; cf. 3:4-5), so also her bridal ornaments are collectively emblematic of the spiritual fidelity and holy conduct of those in the churches who 'overcame'" (p. 287). For a study on the background and significance of the list of gems in Rev 21 see, William S. Reader, "The Twelve Jewels of Revelation 21:19-20: Tradition History and Modern Interpretations," *Journal of Biblical Literature* 100 (1981):433-57.

construction and adornment of buildings seems to have been a practice in the time of the apostles (cf. 1 Cor 3:12). This would have probably been the case in temples and palaces. The adornment of the bride for the wedding was known in the Old Testament and was still practiced during the time of the New Testament among the royalty and the rich.[1]

2. Used as Currency

By the time of the New Testament coins of gold and silver were used as money making it almost unnecessary to use jewelry as currency.[2] The expression "silver and gold" was used in the same way we use the term "money" (Acts 3:6; 20:33).[3] However, in 1 Pet 1:18 the phrase could be referring to objects of gold and silver, possibly in the form of jewelry, used in commercial transactions in the context of the redemption of slaves. Peter is arguing that the price for our redemption was not paid with such valuable, yet perishable, objects but with the blood of Christ (1:19).

This same usage may be present in the instructions Jesus gave to the disciples before sending them out two by two to proclaim the coming of his kingdom: "Do not take along any gold or silver or copper in your belts" (Matt 10:9). However, the parallel passages in Mark and Luke seem to have money in mind rather than precious objects (Mark 6:8; Luke 9:3).

3. Evidence of Wealth

Jewelry appears to be used in several passages as evidence of wealth. The great mystical city of Babylon is personified as a very wealthy woman richly adorned with precious stones and gold (Rev 18:16). James wrote to the rich people of society who oppressed the poor saying, "Your wealth has rotted . . . Your gold and silver are corroded" (5:3). It is also possible that the "gifts of gold" that the Magi gave to Jesus included gold in the form of jewelry (Matt 2:11). In a very special way, pearls were a symbol of great wealth. It would be ridiculous to cast them to the pigs (Matt 7:6). The parable of the Pearl emphasizes this very point (Matt 13:45-46). The merchant in the parable is

---

[1]Fekkes, "Revelation 19-21," p. 284.

[2]See, John W. Betlyon, "Coinage," *Anchor Bible Dictionary*, vol. 1, p. 1086. For a study on the history of coinage consult Colin Kraay, "Coinage," in *The Cambridge Ancient History*, vol. 4, edited by John Boardman, N. G. L. Hammond, D. M. Lewis and M. Ostwald (Cambridge: Cambridge University Press, 1988), pp. 431-45.

[3]G. Schneider, "*Chrysos* Gold," p. 490. The reference would be to coined gold and silver; cf. Bauer, *Lexicon*, p. 897.

a very wealthy person and this is indicated by the fact that he is in the business of buying and selling pearls. He finally invested all he had in a most precious and costly pearl. The great value of this particular pearl testified to his own wealth.

Finally, James mentions the presence in church of a well dressed man "wearing a gold ring" and contrasts him with the poor (2:2), suggesting that the jewelry he wears identifies this person as a wealthy one.[1] He proceeds to reject and condemn discrimination among believers based on material wealth.

4. Symbol of Social Status

The same passage from James could be a good example of the use of jewelry as a symbol of social status. The man well-dressed and wearing a gold ring belongs to the high strata of society but we are not informed about his specific function (2:2).[2] Another case is found in John's description of Jesus at the moment of his second coming. At his return Jesus is wearing "a crown [*stephanos*] of gold on his head" (14:14). The Greek term *stephanos* usually designates a wreath of laurel given to the

---

[1]Scholars disagree on the interpretation of James 2:1-13. One of the questions is related to the use of the term *synagoge*, synagogue. Is it designating the church as a place of worship or the community in a legal session? Another question raised is, Are the two men church members, visitors or newly baptized members? Some believe that this is a church service (e.g. Douglas J. Moo, *James* [Grand Rapids, MI: Eerdmans, 1985], pp. 89-90). While others argue that this is a church business meeting during which the church gathers to judge cases and problems that had arisen among them (R. B. Ward, "Partiality in the Assembly: James 2:2-4," *Harvard Theological Review* 62 [1969]:87-97). The most natural reading of the text would appear to be that the reference is to a regular church meeting. Some argue that these men are Christians or new converts (e.g. Peter Davis, *Commentary on James* [Grand Rapids, MI: Eerdmans, 1982], p. 109), while others call them visitors or unbelievers (e.g. Moo, *James*, p. 89; Martin Dibelius, *James: A Commentary on the Epistle of James* [Philadelphia: Fortress, 1976], p.135). In discussing this case we should keep in mind that James is presenting to the congregation a hypothetical case or at least an illustration. The idea is that if this ever happens during church service you should not allow the person's outward splendor or lack of it determine the way you treat him or her. From that perspective the question of whether he was a church member or not should not even be raised. James is not thinking in those terms (cf. P. U. Maynard-Reid, *Poverty and Wealth in James* [Maryknoll, NY: Orbis, 1987], p. 44; Nancy Jean Vyhmeister, "The Rich Man in James 2: Does Ancient Patronage Illumine the Text?" *Andrews University Seminary Studies* 33 [1995]:277). However, the fact that two men are instructed with respect to where to sit would suggest that they are visitors (Dibelius, *James*, p. 135 n. 63).

[2]"Gold rings also indicated social status in the Roman world. Until the time of Augustus' reign (27 B.C.E. to 14 C.E.), a gold ring on a Roman male citizen's hand meant that he belonged to the second highest order of nobility, the knights" (Cynthia L. Thompson, "Rings of Gold–Neither 'Modest' Nor 'Sensible,'" *Bible Review* 9 [Feb 1993]:29. This man probably was not a Roman knight but seemed to have had an important social role. It has been speculated that he could have been of senatorial rank or a nobleman (Bo Reicke, *The Epistles of James, Peter, and Jude: Introduction Translation and Notes* [Garden City, NY: Doubleday, 1964], p.27). The Greek word *chrusodaktulios* ("gold worn on one's finger") does not seem to designate a signet ring.

winners in the Olympic games, a crown of victory; but it can also refer to a metal crown "as a sign of royal sovereignty."[1] In the passage under consideration Jesus wears this type of crown not only to signal the fact that he is victorious over the enemy but also that he is a royal figure. This idea is explicitly stated in 19:12 where he is described as wearing many diadems, using in this case the Greek term *diadema* which usually designates royal status, kingship and serves to identify Jesus as King of kings (19:16).[2]

Also the twenty four elders have crowns (*stephanos*) of gold on their heads, suggesting that they are coregents with Christ (Rev 4:4).[3] The two women in Revelation seem to be queenly figures and jewelry is used to communicate that idea. The woman representing the people of God wears a symbolic crown of twelve stars (12:1), while the prostituted queen wears the attire and jewelry of a royal personality (17:4).

5. Symbol of Power/Authority

The best example of this particular usage of jewelry is found in the story of the prodigal son in Luke 15:22. When the father sees his son returning home, he orders that he be dressed and that a ring (*daktulios*) be put on his finger. This was a signet ring,[4] "not simply an ornament, but a symbol of authority,"[5] thus indicating that the son was totally re-instituted to the family having all rights as a son. The significance of the ring is underlined by the fact that the father apportioned him his part of the family inheritance before he left home. At the moment of his return the prodigal son had no legal right to inherit anything more or to administer the wealth of his father. By placing the ring on his hand the father was graciously giving to his son a "checking account," and restoring to him the power and authority he enjoyed before leaving the family. Whatever the father had was put at his service.

---

[1]H. Kraft, "*Stephanos* wreath, crown," *Exegetical Dictionary of the NT,* vol. 3, p, 274. On the different functions of crowns in the Greco-Roman society and in the Bible see, Walter Grundmann, "*Stephanos,*" *Theological Dictionary of the NT*, vol 7, edited by Gerhard Friedrich (Grand Rapids, MI: Eerdmans, 1971),pp. 615-33; he also comments that the *stephanos* was worn by kings (p. 620).

[2]C. J. Hemer, "Crown, Scepter, Rod," *New International Dictionary of NT Theology*, vol. 1, edited by Colin Brown (Grand Rapids, MI: Zondervan, 1975), p. 405.

[3]H. Kraft, "*Stephanos,*" p. 274.

[4]Bauer, *Lexicon*, p. 367.

[5]I. Howard Marshall, *The Gospel of Luke: A Commentary on the Greek Text* (Grand Rapids, MI: Eerdmans, 1978), p. 610. Cf. John Nolland, *Luke 9:21-18:34* (Dallas, TX: Word, 1993), p. 785, who rightly argues that this was not the father's signet ring; "the son is being honored, but not made the plenipotentiary of his father."

6. Used as Offerings

There is no explicit use of jewelry as offerings in the New Testament. A possible indirect reference or a similar case may be found in the incident of the Magi. If the gifts of gold they gave Jesus included gold in the form of jewelry, this would be their offering to Jesus as king (Matt 2:11). The gifts were those befitting a king and were a recognition on the part of the Magi that Jesus' messianic kingship was universal.[1] Joseph and Mary now had financial resources for the journey to and for their stay in Egypt.

B. New Testament Attitude Toward Jewelry

As in the Old Testament, jewelry in the New Testament has a restrictive or limited usage. The reference to it as an indicator of material wealth is made in a context where it was accumulated at the expense of the poor and on that basis its value is rejected. The implication would be that as long as wealth is properly obtained and used there is nothing wrong with it. The signet ring does not seem to be rejected possibly because it was a symbol of authority and necessary as a legal instrument. Jewelry is used to indicate social status in the case of kings and queens. These findings are not different at all from what we found in the Old Testament.

The most direct rejection of ornamental jewelry is found in 1 Pet 3:1-6 and 1 Tim 2:9-10. I will make some brief comments on each of these passages anticipating the conclusions of our more careful exegetical analysis found in the next two chapters. According to Peter there is a type of adornment that is incompatible with the Christian life. He illustrates what he has in mind by explicitly mentioning the use of jewelry. This external adornment is contrasted with the true Christian adornment that consists of a gentle and tranquil spirit that determines the quality of the Christian life. By putting on this type of adornment the Christian identifies herself or himself with the aesthetic values of God.

Paul provides for Christians principles to be followed in adorning themselves. Like Peter, he rejects adornment that consists in the use of jewelry and puts the emphasis on the adornment that consists in correct deportment and demeanor; in the principles that should

---

[1]Cf. Donald A. Hagner, *Matthew 1-13* (Dallas, TX: Word, 1993), p. 31. What they gave to Jesus was not simply a gift but an offering because the act of giving was an act of worship. The text explicitly states that the Magi came to worship him (Matt 2:2).

regulate the way Christians are to act and dress. Instead of jewelry Paul calls for the performance of good works that are a reflection of the person's commitment to God. He suggests that the way we adorn ourselves makes a statement on our values as Christians.

The implicit contrast present in the description of the dress and adornment of the two women mentioned in Revelation 12:1 and 17:4 is difficult to interpret. The plain dress of the women who represents the people of God contrasts in a marked way with the greatly ornamented dress of the spiritual prostitute, the mystical Babylon. It is difficult, if not impossible, to determine to what extent the contrast reflects the way Christians adorned themselves during the apostolic church. It may very well be that the vision was not interested at all in those distinctions or that at least it was not illustrating the way women dressed or should dress in the actual life of the church. We suggest the possible connection because Peter and Paul recommended the same absence of ornamental jewelry for Christian women that we find in the case of the woman in Rev 12:1.

Undoubtedly, the contrast in the way these two women were dressed and adorned is significant and could have been instructive for the church as it sought to define and establish its identity in society as the instrument of God. But the fact that she stands for the people of God through the centuries could illustrate the simplicity of the dress of those who form part of the people of God. The contrast is indeed between the true worshippers of God and the false ones.

C. Conclusion

The New Testament materials on jewelry are in fundamental agreement with what we found in the Old Testament in suggesting a very limited use of jewelry. In the New Testament we find the case of jewelry for personal ornamentation explicitly addressed and rejected. Jewelry as a symbol of royalty is used by Christ, who is described as wearing a crown of gold. In his case it represents victory and universal sovereignty.

Christians embrace a life of personal commitment to the Lord and adorn themselves with the content and fruits of the Christian faith. Yes, they should be interested in adorning themselves in modesty and decency, taking care of their demeanor as it expresses itself in conduct and personal appearance. But such concern should be put at the service of the Lord and the communication of the Christian message.

The Christian lives in hope anticipating the restoration of all things through the power of the Lord and the moment when Christ, the King of kings, will share his royal power with his people (Rev 5:10), to whom he says: "Be faithful, even to the point of death, and I will give you the crown of life" (2:10).

1 PETER 3:1-6:
AN EXEGETICAL ANALYSIS

A. Contextual Considerations

This passage belongs to a section of the epistle in which Peter is discussing how Christians should relate to other persons, especially with those who are not part of the Christian community. They are asked to respect the authority of kings and governors (2:13-17), and slaves are advised to submit themselves to their masters (2:18-25). The objective is to "silence the ignorant talk of foolish men" (v. 15), who were seeking opportunities to oppose the Christian church.

Next, Peter addresses the married women of the church and their husbands (3:1-7). Most of the advice is directed to wives because a number of them were married to unbelievers. They are asked to submit themselves to their husbands with the purpose of witnessing to them through their behavior hoping that they might be converted to the gospel. Submitting to the husband seems to be explained in terms of living a life of "purity and reverence" (3:2; a literal translation would be, "Seeing/observing your pure behavior in fear"), devoid of verbal conflicts by testifying to their husbands through their Christian behavior. The adjective *hagnos* ("pure") is most probably emphasizing here moral purity but it also includes the idea of rejecting evil in general, i.e. purity of life.[1] This same quality of life was expected from all believers and from church leaders (Phil 4:8; 1 Tim 5:22). "In fear" does not mean that the wife is to be afraid of her husband but it rather refers to her fear or commitment to the Lord (cf. 1:17; 2:17,18). This is supported by verse 6 where they are encouraged to do what is right and not be afraid of anyone.[2] Purity in the fear of the Lord means that the pure behavior of the wives "arises out of reverence to God."[3]

B. Analysis of the Passage

1. Outward Adornment

The wives' primary commitment to the Lord is to express itself in the way they adorn themselves. In 3:3,4 we find a contrast between personal

---

[1]See Ceslas Spicq, *Les épitres de Saint Pierre* (Paris: J. Gabalda, 1966), p.117, and H. Balz, "*Hagnos* pure, undefiled, chaste," *Exegetical Dictionary of the NT*, vol. 1, p. 22.

[2]J. Ramsey Michaels, *1 Peter* (Waco, TX: Word, 1988), p. 158.

[3]Ernest Best, *1 Peter* (Grand Rapids, MI: Eerdmans, 1971), p. 125; see also Norman Hillyer, *1 and 2 Peter, Jude* (Peabody, MS: Hendrickson, 1992), p. 93.

adornment which is external, and not pleasing to the Lord, and that which is internal and pleasing to the Lord. The apostle mentions three cases which illustrate the type of adornment he considers improper for the Christian woman. The first one is the "braiding of hair" (*emplokes trichon*). This is a technical phrase which describes a particular type of hairdressing common during the time of Peter particularly among wealthy ladies.[1] It was an elaborated braided hairstyle unusually high which was sometimes "held up by a wire or lacquer."[2] Undoubtedly, "these coiffures required leisure to construct them, sometimes by means of a curling iron and often with the help of a slave."[3] The hair was in some cases decorated "with countless gold spangles almost entirely hiding the hair, glittering and tinkling with every movement of the head."[4] Strabo describes a people who "beautify their appearance by braiding their hair, growing beards, wearing golden ornaments . . . And only rarely can you see them touching one another in walking, for fear that the adornment of their hair may not remain intact."[5]

Peter rejects the adornment that consists of putting on gold ornaments (*ho exothen . . . peritheseos chrusion*, lit. "The exterior [adornment] of putting on gold [objects]"). These would include necklaces, earrings, bracelets and ornaments of gold worn round the hair.[6] It was not uncommon to find women throughout the Roman Empire loaded with all kind of jewelry. Many of them, according to some historians, looked like ambulatory jewelry shops.[7] Peter finds this to be incompatible with the Christian spirit.

Finally, the apostle mentions the "wearing of fine clothing" (*enduseos himation*, lit. "putting on of garments"). It is obvious that Peter has in mind certain type of clothing and not clothing in general. Hence the translations "fine

---

[1] This should not be interpreted to mean that women in the church came mainly from the wealthy class. But it certainly suggests that there were wealthy ladies in the church.

[2] Cynthia L. Thompson, "Hairstyles, Head-coverings, and St. Paul: Portraits from Roman Corinth," *Biblical Archaeolgist* 51 (June 1988):108.

[3] Ibid.

[4] Hillyer, *1 Peter*, p. 95. The hair was often "intertwined with chains of gold or strings of pearl" (Daniel C. Arichea and Eugene A. Nida, *A Translator's Handbook on the First Letter from Peter* [New York: United Bible Societies, 1980], p. 90).

[5] *Geography* 17.3.7.

[6] See Spicq, *Pierre*, p. 118.

[7] U. O. Paoli, *Vita Romana* (Bruges-Paris: 1955), p. 199.

clothing" (RSV), "grand robes," and others.[1] The word *himation*, rendered "clothing," originally designated a specific piece of garment, namely, the outer garment "formed by an oblong piece of cloth worn above the *chiton* [tunic, undergarment];"[2] although it was also used to refer to garments in a more general way.[3] This type of dress could be very simple or very sophisticated becoming an adornment and establishing social distinctions (cf. Luke 7:25).

Garment has a symbolic meaning in the Bible. It is interesting to observe that in the Scriptures "the condition and inner workings of a person are expressed by his or her appearance, which includes clothing. This is the case of the shining garments of the transfigured Jesus (Mark 9:3 par. Matt 17:2), of the power-filled cloak of the Savior (Mark 5:27, 28, 30 par.; 6:56 par. Matt 14:36), and of the 'soft' clothing of the 'indolent' aristocrats (Luke 7:25)."[4] Peter is interested in a type of dress that is compatible with Christian values and spirit.

2. Rejection of Jewelry or Improper Use?

Having defined to some extent what Peter had in mind in his description of the adornment he is rejecting we should now determine whether he was condemning the use of jewelry or only an improper use of it. The prevailing opinion among commentators is that Peter was not condemning a moderate use of jewelry. His point, it is argued, "is rather that the attraction of the Christian wife to her pagan husband is to consist not in external adornment but in the more important internal qualities outlined in the following verse."[5]

Another writer has suggested that "it is incorrect, therefore, to use this text to prohibit women from braiding their hair or wearing gold jewelry, for by the same reasoning one would have to prohibit 'putting on clothing'. Peter's point is not that any of these are forbidden, but that they should not be a woman's 'adorning', her source of beauty."[6] The Greek sentence, it has

---

[1]Bo Reicke, *The Epistles of James, Peter, and Jude* (Golden City, NY: Doubleday, 1964), p. 100.

[2]Bauer, *Lexicon*, p. 829.

[3]W. Radl, "*Himation* garment, cloak," in *Exegetical Dictionary of the NT*, vol. 2, p. 187; cf. Ulrich Wilckens, "*Stole,*" *Theological Dictionary of the NT*, 7:690.

[4]Radl, "*Himation,*" p. 188. On the symbolism of clothing see Edgar Haulette, *Symbolique du vetement selon la Bible* (Aubier: Editions Motaigne, 1966).

[5]Achtemeier, *1 Peter*, p. 212. Cf. Michaels, *1 Peter*, p. 160.

[6]Grudem, *1 Peter*, p. 140. This line of reasoning is supported also by Achtemeier, *1 Peter*, pp. 212, 213.

been argued, "might well be translated: 'Your beauty should *not so much* come from outward adornment . . . *but rather* it should be that of your inner self.'"[1] This translation is probably based on the argument that in a Greek sentence the combination "not [*ou*] . . . but [*alla*]" sometimes could mean "'not so much . . . as' in which the first element is not entirely negated but only toned down"[2] (Matt 4:4; John 11:52; 1 Pet 2:18). But it is also true that *alla* ("but") "appears most frequently as the contrary to a preceding *ou*" ("not"),[3] and, more important, whenever "no" (*ou*) is denying a phrase in the imperative, as is the case in 1 Pet 3:3, the following "but" (*alla*) introduces the contrasting subject and it simply means "not (this) . . . but on the contrary . . ."[4]

What then should we conclude? There are several things that can be said concerning Peter's intention in this passage. First, we have here a prohibition voiced in Peter's apostolic authority.[5] He is clearly contrasting two types of behaviors or values and is rejecting one and promoting the other. But this is more than promotion. He is establishing what is right, what is expected of a Christian woman, and what is not

---

[1]Marshall, *1 Peter*, p. 101.

[2]F. Blass, A. Debrunner, and Robert W. Funk, *A Greek Grammar of the NT and Other Early Christian Literature* (Chicago, IL: University of Chicago Press, 1961), p. 233. In most of those cases the phrase is "not only [*ou monon*] . . . but also [*alla kai*]." Although in a few cases the simple formula "not . . . but" means "not so much . . . as" (e.g. Mark 9:37).

[3]Ibid., p. 232.

[4]W. Radl has indicated that when *alla* ("but") follows a negation it means "on the contrary, rather" ("*Alla* rather, but," *Exegetical Dictionary NT*, vol. 1, p. 61). What we have in 1 Pet 3:3 is a case of phrase negation followed by a contrasting phrase introduced by *alla* (see Stanley E. Porter, *Idioms of the Greek NT* [Sheffield: Academic Press, 1994], p. 282). I checked the use of the formula with present imperatives in the New Testament and I did not find a single case in which the phrase meant "not so much . . . as," or "not only . . . but."

[5]Karl Hermann Schelkle, *Die Petrusbriefe. Der Judasbrief* (Freiburg: Herder, 1961), p. 89, comments that "the letter condemns with a very strong judgment external ornaments (3,3), and requires to the same extent the inner beauty." Peter uses a third person plural imperative which is usually translated into English as an imperative of permission ("let . . ."). This is understandable because we do not have in English a third person imperative. Here the remarks of a Greek grammarian are pertinent: "Greek has imperative forms in the second and third person, singular and plural. Whereas the second person is similar to the English form when translated, the third person imperative requires what has sometimes been labeled a permissive sense (let. . .). However, any permissive sense is a phenomenon of English translation, not Greek. The third person Greek imperative is as strongly directive as the second person" (Porter, *Idioms*, p. 55). The present imperative is used in Greek for commands and prohibitions (Ibid., p. 56; and James Hope Moulton and Nigel Turner, *A Grammar of the NT Greek III: Syntax* [Edinburgh: T. & T. Clark, 1963], pp.74, 75). In 1 Pet 3:3 we have a combination of both ideas. In the first clause we find the negative imperative, "*Let not* your adornment *be* . . ." (a prohibition) followed by a second clause in which the same imperative is implicit and functions as a command ("but rather [*let it be*] the hidden . . .").

acceptable in the community of believers. Whether his views are culturally conditioned or not will be discussed later on.

Second, Peter does not seem to be totally rejecting personal adornment. As we noticed, he is not condemning hairdressing but a certain type of hairdressing. The same applies to clothing. The noun "adornment" (Greek, *kosmos*) designates in Greek literature "arrangement, order,"[1] and then beauty or adornment.[2] In the NT it is only in 1 Pet 3:3 that this noun means "adornment" and its use does not suggest that there is something intrinsically wrong with adorning oneself. The real issue is the rejection of a certain type of adornment. Christians are to take proper care of their appearance but it should not be in conflict with Christian values and the purpose of a Christian life.

Finally, Peter *is rejecting the use of jewelry as an exterior adornment and probably also as a sign of social* status. The text does not address the use of jewelry for other functional purposes (e.g. as signet seals), although Peter is aware of the fact that gold has other proper usages besides adornment (e.g. as currency; 1 Pet 1:18). These distinctions are important if we want to correctly understand the standard that he is setting up in this passage for the believer. Peter's position is compatible with what we found in the OT.

3. Source of Peter's Command

Our next question has to do with the motivation behind this command. Is Peter simply promoting the values of the society in which he lived? To what extent is what he is saying valid for the church of all ages? A number of scholars argue that Peter's views were motivated by specific problems the church was confronting in the first century and, therefore, they are no longer applicable to the church today because it exists in a different social environment. These scholars put the emphasis on the principle that Peter is promoting and not on the specific examples used by him to illustrate the principle. According to them Peter is calling Christians to control their

---

[1]H. Balz, "*Kosmos* world, universe; ornament; totality," *Exegetical Dictionary of the NT*, vol. 2, p.309.

[2]Hermann Sasse, "*Kosmeo, kosmos*," *Theological Dictionary of the NT*, vol. 3, p. 869. The verb *kosmeo* is used in the NT more often than the noun to express the idea of beauty and adornment (p. 867); see also H. Balz, "*Kosmeo* put in order; decorate, adorn," *Exegetical Dictionary of the NT*, vol. 2, p. 309; Ceslas Spicq, *Lexicon*, vol. 2, pp. 330-35.

desire for ostentation and luxury,[1] to promote the principle of simplicity in dress[2] and freedom from dependence on outward show.[3]

Those scholars moved away from the specific examples motivated in part by the fact that in the Greco-Roman tradition it was believed that proper female attire should be characterized by simplicity and modesty and consequently the use of jewelry was discouraged.[4] Peter was writing to women who had become Christians rejecting the religion of their husbands, something considered by society at large to be an act of insubordination on the part of the wives.[5] His advice to them is based on a code of behavior common in the Greco-Roman world for wives and has the purpose of showing that, when it comes to their behavior and the way they dress and adorn themselves, Christian wives support the moral values of their husbands. This reading of the text makes Peter's specific prohibition culturally conditioned and to some extent irrelevant to Western culture today. It is then concluded that the biblical interpreter could only transfer to the church today the principles behind the specific examples.

Obviously, we have to raise the question of the value of this approach to the biblical text. There is a fact that we must accept, namely, we do have Greek and Roman writers from around the time of Peter giving very similar advice to ladies in the Roman society. It is indeed probable that Peter may have been acquainted with the teachings of those non-Christian moralists. But the question remains, Did they provide for Peter the values that he is promoting? Is he asking the wives of non-Christians to adjust their deportment to what was expected from them by society at large?

To the first question we should give a negative answer. Peter himself tells us the source of his prohibition. He specifically makes reference to the "the holy women" of the OT. They, not the teachings of the Roman moralists,

---

[1] Schelkle, *Petrusbriefe*, p. 89 argues that Peter's command is socially and temporally conditioned but finds here a call for Christians to control their appetite for ostentation.

[2] See, Davids, *1 Peter*, p.118, who comments that even though the passage should not be used to legislate feminine dress the emphasis on simplicity in dress should be taken seriously by the church.

[3] See Wolfgang Schrage, *The Ethics of the NT* (Philadelphia: Fortress, 1988), p. 276, who writes, "Although we may realize that this attitude is historically conditioned and 'puritanical,' we must not lose sight of its true intention: freedom from dependence on outward show and luxury." Cf. Leonhard Goppelt, *A Commentary on 1 Peter* (Grand Rapids, MI: Eerdmans, 1993), pp. 220-21.

[4] For references to Greek and Roman writers see Achtemeier, 1 Peter, p. 212. The best discussion of this subject is found in David L. Balch, *Let Wives be Submissive: The Domestic Code in 1 Peter* (Chico, CA: Scholars, 1981), pp. 80-114.

[5] See Balch, *Wives*, pp. 88-90.

provide for him the model to be followed by the Christian wives. It is even probable that the apostle also has in mind Isa 3:18-24. His "frequent use of Isaiah in the preceding verses, especially 2:22-25, makes knowledge of this passage likely."[1] Yet, he does not quote from an abstract teaching but points to people who incorporated it into their lives. Furthermore, Peter indicates that true spiritual virtues, the inner adornment of the Christian, are "precious" in God's sight (3:4); He "regards and values them highly."[2] This is the ultimate criterion for proper adornment, not what is socially convenient. The implications are quite clear. The adornment used by holy women in a different time and culture is considered by Peter to be valid for the Christian ladies of his day and continues to be precious before the Lord. He does not separate the concrete example from the principle itself. The standard he is setting does not seem to be culturally determined.

The fact that Roman society promoted the same values the church is promoting gives Peter the opportunity to remind the community that Christians can use this to promote the respectability of Christianity in a pagan environment and that it could also become an instrument to win the non-Christian husbands to the gospel. He appears to be saying that it is not the function of Christianity to upset social order but rather to support it whenever possible.[3] Peter's instructions on proper adornment belong to the Christian tradition (cf. 1 Tim 2:9-10).[4] It could be said that Peter has an apologetic purpose in that according to him Christian morality is not incompatible with the highest moral values of a pagan society.[5] The moral teachings of Greek and Roman writers do not determine the content of the teaching of Peter but provide a reason for its inclusion in the Epistle. The shared values contribute to a reduction of tensions with the Roman society.

---

[1]Achtemeier, *1 Peter*, p. 211. See also, Bigg, *Peter*, p.153. Edward Gordon Selwyn comments, "The three kinds of outward ornament here [1 Pet 3:3] specified are coiffure, jewellery, and dress, all are alluded to in . . . Is. iii. 18-24" (*The First Epistle of Saint Peter* [London: Macmillian, 1955], p. 183. Yet he argues that the passage was not in Peter's mind.

[2]Spicq, *Lexicon*, vol. 3, p. 135.

[3]However, it has been pointed out that Peter also criticizes "traditional Roman culture as (1) 'unjust' for slaves, and (2) too restrictive for wives, who were exhorted not to allow the husbands to 'terrify' them (1 Pet. 3:6)" (David Balch, "Early Christian Criticism of Patriarchal Authority: 1 Peter 2:11-3:12," *Union Seminary Quarterly Review* 39 [1984]:170).

[4]Otto Knoch, *Der erste und zweite Petrusbrief. Der Judasbrief* (Regensburg: Verlag Friedrich Pustet, 1990), p. 89, and Norbert Brox, *Der erste Petrusbrief* (Neukirchen-Vluyn: Neukirchener Verlag, 1979), p. 145.

[5]Cf. Davids, *1 Peter*, p. 118.

4. Nature of True Adornment

The true adornment is "the hidden person of the heart with the imperishable jewel of a gentle [*praeos*] and quiet [*hesuchiou*] spirit, which in God's sight is precious" (3:4). The contrast the apostle is making is not between the visible and the invisible dimensions of a person; there is no dualism here. In the phrase "the hidden person of the heart" the noun "heart" explains what is meant by "the hidden person," i.e. the center of thought and action.[1] We can then suggest that "'the hidden person' is not the inner side of the person, but the whole human being as it is determined from within, 'from the heart,' i.e. from believing thoughts and desires."[2] This person is visible to God and expresses himself or herself through external actions and dispositions visible to others.[3]

Peter indicates that the beauty of the heart expresses itself in "the imperishable jewel of a gentle and quiet spirit." The implication is that external adornment is perishable and belongs to the sphere of the ephemeral lacking permanent value (cf. 1 Peter 1:18). "Gentle" (Gr. *prays*) as an adjective designates the absence of violence based on trust in the Lord.[4] It describes the poor, even the oppressed who have nothing to show except their reliance on God and consequently wait patiently on Him (Matt 5:5). There is an absence of pride in such individuals.[5] Their dependence on God makes them gentle, mild, and kind even under difficult circumstances.[6] This gentle and mild spirit characterized Jesus (Matt 11:29) and he expected it to be also a mark of those who would follow him, whether male or female

---

[1]See Achtemeier, *1 Peter*, p. 213; Michaels. *1 Peter*, p. 161.

[2]Goppelt, *1 Peter*, p. 221.

[3]Achtemeier, *1 Peter*, p. 213, states, "The 'secret person' in this context refers not so much to the general inner aspect of the human being as it does to the person who is determined by a faith that is visible directly only to God (cf. Matt 6:4, 6, 8, 18), and that is apparent to other human beings only by way of external acts."

[4]H, Frankemolle, "*Praus* gentle, kind, mild," *Exegetical Dictionary of the NT*, vol. 3, p. 147.

[5]D. G. Burke, "Meek; Meekness," *International Standard Bible Encyclopedia*, vol. 3, p. 307, writes, "Meekness is the opposite of pride, for pride is the arrogant reliance on self alone rather than on God."

[6]See Spicq, *Lexicon*, vol. 3, p. 168. His discussion of the use of the term *prays* in Greek writers is worth quoting: "The *praos* has a mild look (Plutarch, *De cohib, ira* 6.456 a), a smiling countenance (4.455 a-b), a soft voice (Xenophon, *Symp.* 1.10), a tranquil demeanor (*praotes poreias*, Per. 5.1; Fab. 17.7); is accommodating and affable (*Arist.* 23.1), courteous (*Alex.* 58.8), charming and gracious (*Ages.* 20.7; *Aem.* 3.6), but also quiet and reserved (*De fract. amor.* 16.487 c), and at the same time easygoing and welcoming toward all (*Praec. ger. rei publ.* 32.823f). His character is conciliatory. He does not like quarrels (*Lyc.* 25.4). . ."

(Matt 5:5; cf. the use of the noun [*praytes*, "gentleness"] in Gal 5:23; Eph 4:2; and Col 3:12). Such spirit or disposition should control the behavior of wives and believers in general.

The "quiet spirit" reinforces the idea of absence of conflict in the Christian life. The adjective *hesuchios* means "quiet, tranquil." A "'quiet' spirit is the ideal both for the Christian community (1Tim 2:2) as well as for individual Christians (1 Thess 4:11; 2 Thess 3:12),"[1] that is to say, it would be a characteristic of both, man and woman. As a Christian virtue it designates a disposition of tranquility and peacefulness in the midst of potential or real conflicts, possibly based on the inner tranquility produced by being at peace with God.[2] The absence of this virtue generates personal and social turmoil.[3] "A gentle and tranquil spirit" will do more on behalf of the Christian wife of an unbeliever than any external adornment. But more important, through this type of adornment women are identifying themselves with and incorporating into their lives God's value system.[4]

C. Conclusion

We can conclude that the prohibition of jewelry as adornment is not determined by local factors confronted by the church during the time of Peter. It is not culturally determined. He is describing for the church what

---

[1]Achtemeier, *1 Peter*, p. 214.

[2]Spicq, *Lexicon*, vol. 2, points out that in the OT this tranquility is given by the Lord to His people and it includes "interior calm, as opposed to anxiety and fear"(p. 180); cf. C. H. Peisker, "*Hesychios* quiet, tranquil," *Exegetical Dictionary of the NT*, vol. 2, p. 125.

[3]Cf. M. J. Harris, "*Hesychia*," *New International Dictionary of NT Theology*, vol. 3, Colin Brown, ed. (Grand Rapids, MI: Zondervan, 1978), pp. 111-12.

[4]Some scholars have argued that there is a direct connection between submission to the husband and the rejection of jewelry by women (David M. Scholer, "Women's Adornment: Some Historical and Hermeneutical Observations on the NT Passages," *Daughters of Sarah* 6 [January/February 1980]:3-6). The idea would be that by not wearing jewelry a woman indicated her submission to her husband. It is interesting to observe that Peter begins and ends his message to the women of the church with the topic of submission to their husbands (3:1, 5). However, even if it was considered improper in the Greco-Roman society for a woman to wear jewelry because she would be showing no respect to her husband (this is far from certain; see below our discussion on 1 Tim 2:9-10), this does not seem to have been Peter's concern and he does not explicitly address it. He develops, as we have seen, important theological concerns in association with proper adornment and their implication for Christian experience and witnessing. Peter is dealing with two different but related subjects–submission to the non-Christian husband and proper adornment–but he is not defining one on the basis of the other. It has been suggested that perhaps the inward spiritual adornment that Peter recommends would probably include submission and respect to the husband (Beare, *1 Peter*, p. 30), but this is not clearly indicated in the text. But even if that were the case it would not be correct to argue that the reason for Peter's rejection of external adornment consisting of jewelry was simply for the ladies to demonstrate that they were submitted to their husbands.

the Lord has always expected from His people since the time of the OT. What was proper in terms of adornment for the "holy women" of Israel is still valid for the Christian believer.

One can extrapolate from the text different possible reasons for the prohibition. First, there seems to be a concern for the correct use of financial resources. Yet, this does not seem to us to be one of the primary reasons for the injunction against certain types of external adornment. At least the apostle does not explicitly make an issue out of this and the context does not seem to point to it as a significant element in the development of the topic. Second, since the adornments described by Peter are the ones usually worn by wealthy ladies it would be right to suggest that they had also the purpose of establishing social distinctions between the rich and the poor. If this is the case, then Peter is also rejecting the use of jewelry as a sign of social status among believers. But again this is not clearly stated in the text.

Third, the contrast between the external and hidden adornments reveals quite clearly the rationale for the rejection of the first. The adornment that is being rejected is considered by Peter not to be an expression of a "gentle spirit." If our understanding of that phrase is correct then what he is suggesting is that there is a type of external adornment that is an expression of pride and self-reliance instead of being an expression of the person's submission and dependence on the Lord. It is therefore logical for the Christian to reject one and put on the other. When contrasted with a "tranquil spirit" external adornment becomes an expression of a restless attitude, a symbol of a need, even a quest for inner peace that is unsatisfied but which should have been fully met through the gospel. Hence such adornment is incompatible with the fruits of the Christian message.

Fourth, Peter refers to the women of the Old Testament, who used proper adornment, as "holy women." In this particular case "holy" probably means that they belonged to the Lord, that they were part of the people of God. Their adornment had the purpose of setting boundaries by establishing religious distinctions with respect to other nations. The implication is that true adornment was an expression of their commitment to the Lord.

Finally, Peter rejects a certain type of external adornment because it is not "precious in the sight of the Lord." The implication is that Christians are to identify themselves with what the Lord considers to be valuable. In the process they are developing attitudes and aesthetic taste that correspond to those of God. The *imitatio dei* is operative even in the way Christians adorn themselves. After all, God does not wear jewelry.

1 TIMOTHY 2:9,10:
AN EXEGETICAL ANALYSIS

A. Contextual Considerations

Paul is giving instruction concerning proper worship practice and behavior. First he encourages (*parakaleo*, "to exhort") believers to pray for all people, particularly political leaders, in order for the church to "lead a quiet and peaceable life, godly and respectful in every way" (2:2). This is something the Lord expects from his people and is based on the fact that he desires to save everybody and has made this possible through the sacrifice of Christ Jesus (2:3-6). Paul is himself a preacher and teacher of this message. Second, the apostle gives instruction to men concerning the proper attitude during prayer. He desires (*boulomai*) that they pray in holiness and without anger or quarreling (2:8). The verb *boulomai* may give the impression that Paul is giving general advice, expressing a wish. But it really means "want, persist in, insist on, command," and in this passage "it has an imperative ring."[1]

Next, Paul addresses the women of the church. The question is whether he is dealing here with their attitude during prayer or with proper conduct in general. Verse 9 begins, "Likewise [*hosautos*] women . . ." This has led some to suggest that the verbs used at the beginning of verse 8 should be supplied here: "Likewise [I desire] women [to pray] . . ."[2] The term "likewise" suggests that a thought from the previous verse is being developed or applied to the advice being given to women. If we look at the combination of the verbs used at the beginning of verse 8 and at the verb used in verse 9 we would be able to determine what the apostle had in mind. In v. 8 we find a first person singular verb followed by an infinitive verb that rounds up the thought: "I desire [*boulomai*] . . . [men] . . . to pray [*proseuchesthai*]." The only verb used in v. 9 is an infinitive requiring that we transfer from the previous verse the finite verb "I desire." The grammatical construction would then be the same as in the previous verse: "[I desire] . . . [women] . . . to adorn [*kosmein*]

---

[1]H.-J. Ritz, "*Boulomai* want, persist in," *Exegetical Dictionary of the NT*, vol. 1, p. 225.

[2]E.g. Martin Dibelius and Hans Conzelmann, *The Pastoral Epistles* (Philadelphia: Fortress, 1972), p.45; Cesla Spicq, *Saint Paul: Les Epitres Pastorales* (Paris: Gabalda, 1969), p. 66; Thomas C. Oden, *First and Second Timothy and Titus* (Louisville, TN: Knox, 1989), p. 93; Craig S. Keener, *Paul, Women and Wives: Marriage and Women's Ministry in the Letters of Paul* (Peabody, Massachusetts: Hendrickson, 1992), p. 102; and Nancy J. Vyhmeister, "Proper Church Behavior in 1 Tim 2:8-15," in *Women in Ministry: Biblical and Historical Perspectives*, Nancy J. Vyhmeister, ed. (Berrien Springs, MI: Andrews University Press, 1998), p. 340.

themselves . . ."[1] This suggests that the subject is no longer prayer but proper adornment.

The question is whether the adornment described in the following verses is the one exclusively required for the worship service in church[2] or also to that expected from the Christian women outside the church. One cannot deny that Paul is addressing the church in worship, but neither can one affirm that his instruction is limited only to that context. For instance, should prayers for all men be made only while in church? Are "good works" (2:10) to be performed only at church? The obvious answer is no. While giving these instructions Paul had primarily the worship service in mind but his instructions were relevant for the Christian life in general. This applies also to the instruction he gives concerning the proper adornment of women.[3]

B. Analysis of the Passage

The general structure of 1 Tim 2:9,10 is very simple:

A. *Proper adornment (v. 9a)*

      B. *Improper adornment (v.9b)*

A. *Proper adornment (v. 10).*

There is a movement from general principles (v. 9a), to specific examples (v. 9b), to spiritual adornment (v. 10). The first and last are affirmed and the middle one is rejected. The subject of discussion is personal adornment as indicated by the verb *kosmein*, "decorate, adorn."

1. Defining Proper Adornment

Paul begins with a statement of the principles involved on the subject of personal appearance: "Women should adorn themselves modestly and

---

[1]Sometimes when *hosautos* is used in enumerations "the verb can be omitted and supplied from the context (. . . 1 Tim 2:9: *boulomai* . . .)" (Horst Balz and Gerhard Schneider, "*Hosautos* similarly, in the same way," *Exegetical Dictionary of the NT*, vol. 3, p. 510).

[2]Thus, e.g. Fred D. Gealy, "The First and Second Epistles of Timothy and Titus: Introduction and Exegesis," *Interpreter's Bible*, vol 11, G. A Buttrick, ed. (Nashville, TN: Abingdon, 1955), p. 404; and Ralph Earle, "1 Timothy," *Expositor's Bible Commentary*, vol. 11, F. E. Gaebelein, ed. (Grand Rapids, MI: Zondervan, 1978), p. 360.

[3]George W. Knight III, *Commentary on the Pastoral Epistles* (Grand Rapids, MI: Eerdmans, 1992), pp. 130-31, argued the same way and concluded, "Paul's instructions to women, like the preceding instructions to men, are related to the context of the gathered Christian community but are not restricted to it. Men must always live holy lives that avoid wrath and dispute, particularly in connection with prayer for others; women are always to live in accord with their profession of godliness, dressing modestly and discreetly." Cf. Donald Guthrie, *The Pastoral Epistles* (Grand Rapids, MI: Eerdmans, 1990), p. 84, who comments, "The advice given seems to be general and we must therefore suppose that Paul turned from his immediate purpose in order to make wider observations about women's demeanour."

sensibly in seemly apparel" (RSV). In Greek the phrase "in seemly apparel" is located before "modestly and sensibly" suggesting that what follows clarifies or develops the meaning of "in seemly apparel." The meaning of this phrase is difficult to ascertain. Bible versions translate the Greek in different ways: "to dress modestly" (NIV), "dress in becoming manner" (NEB), "in suitable clothing" (NRSV), "must deport themselves properly" (NAB), "adorn themselves with proper clothing" (NASB), "to wear suitable clothes" (NJB).

The phrase *en katastole kosmio* ("in seemly apparel") is governed by the verb "to adorn" (*kosmein*). *Katastole* ("apparel") has two possible meanings in Greek, making its usage here a little unclear. It designates the person's "demeanor, deportment" which expresses itself (1) in proper conduct and disposition or (2) in the exterior appearance. In the first case it could be translated "demeanor, conduct" and in the second "clothing."[1] The meaning "'clothes, clothing' derives from the fact that decorum finds a first visible impression in clothing."[2] Since in 1 Tim 2:9b clothing is mentioned some translators concluded that the word *katastole* means here "clothing, dress, apparel." But the mention of "good works" as the true adornment of women (v. 10) suggests that the principal idea is one of conduct, proper deportment or demeanor. But perhaps it is probably better to recognize that *katastole* refers here to demeanor or deportment as proper conduct and disposition and also to its expression in clothing.[3]

The second Greek term, rendered "seemly" in RSV, is *kosmios*, an adjective derived from *kosmos* ("order," "adornment"), and means "disciplined," "well-mannered," "honorable."[4] In secular Greek this term is used to describe a self-disciplined, well-mannered person who is regarded by others as respectable and honorable.[5] These ideas fit very well the

---

[1]Bauer, *Lexicon*, p. 420.

[2]K. H. Rengstorf, "*Katastello, Katastole,*" in *Theological Dictionar of the NT*, vol. 7, p. 595.

[3]With Arndt and Gingrich, *Lexicon*, p. 420; Rengstorf, "*Katastole,*" p. 596; Gerhard Schneider, "*Katastole* demeanor, bearing; appearance," *Exegetical Dictionary of the New Testament*, vol. 2, p. 269; Dibelius and Conzelmann, *Pastoral*, pp. 45-46; Donald Guthrie, *The Pastoral Epistles* (Grand Rapids, MI: Eerdmans, 1990), p. 84; Alan Padgett, "Wealthy Women at Ephesus: 1 Timothy 2:8-15 in Social Context," *Interpretation* 41 (1987):22.

[4]Hermann Sasse, "*Kosmios,*" *Theological Dictionary of the NT*, vol. 3, p. 896.

[5]Ibid., p. 895 and Gerhard Schneider, "*Kosmios* respectable, honorable," *Exegetical Dictionary of the NT*, vol. 2, p. 309.

passage under discussion. Paul is, then, saying that women are to adorn themselves "in respectable/honorable demeanor," which expresses itself in morally upright conduct and modest external appearance, i.e. clothing. The emphasis seems to be on the impact that such deportment on the part of women would have upon others; they will be regarded as respectable ladies.

The next phrase, "modestly and sensibly," is introduced by the preposition *meta* ("with"), which was not translated in the RSV, and indicates "the fashion in which the action is accomplished;"[1] in this case the action is that of adorning oneself. The terms "modestly [*aidos*] and sensibly [*sophrosune*]" are rich in meaning and are also used in Greek literature in conjunction with *kosmios* ("honorable").[2] *Aidos* ("modesty, respect") comes from a verb that means "to fear, respect." This fear was considered to be the "respectful and secret fear that one feels toward oneself,"[3] a feeling of shame that is experienced after breaking the limits of propriety and that could be equated with what we would call pudor or modesty.[4] Greeks considered it to be a virtue and described it as "a restraint, a dignity, a modesty, or a discretion that keeps one from excess; thus a self-respect and a sense of honor that is often identified with modesty."[5] It is the virtue of *aidos* that "keeps one from committing an act unworthy of oneself, makes one avoid that which is base."[6] In fact, this virtue is the opposite of arrogance (*hybris*).[7] It is this cluster of ideas that we should keep in mind when the term is translated "modesty" in 1 Tim 2:9.

---

[1]Spicq, *Lexicon*, 3:362; cf. Knight, *Pastoral*, p. 134: "The prepositional phrase introduced by *meta* denotes the state of mind or attitude necessary for one to be concerned about modesty and thus to dress modestly."

[2]Ibid., p. 896; and Spicq, *Lexicon*, vol. 2, p. 332 who writes, "The connection between *kosmios, sophron (sophrosune)*, and *aidos* is so constant in the Hellenistic period that it must be considered a literary topos from Xenophon [b. 431BC] on; its point is always to emphasize conformity to the rules of decency and modesty, the control of attitude and bearing: beauty is joined in its possessor 'with modesty and reserve, *met' aidous kai sophrosynes* (Xenophon, *Symp.* 1.8; cf. *Cyr.* 8.1.31)."

[3]Spicq, *Lexicon*, vol. 1, p. 41.

[4]See R. Bultmann, "*Aidos*," *Theological Dictionary of the NT*, vol. 1, p. 169; H.-G. Link and E. Tiedke, "Shame, Respect: *Aidos*," *New International Dictionary of NT Theology*, vol. 1, p. 351.

[5]Spicq, *Lexicon*, 1:42.

[6]Ibid., p. 43.

[7]Bultmann, "*Aidos*," p. 169.

The term *sophrosune* ("reasonableness, decency"), translated "sensibly" in the RSV, comes from a verb whose basic meaning is "to be of sound mind."[1] The diversity of usages of this noun in Greek writings makes it difficult to find an appropriate English word for it.[2] Among its possible meanings we find "prudence, moderation, sound judgment, decency, self-control, mastery of the passions."[3] The most common ideas associated with it by the period of the NT seem to have been self-control and reasonableness, suggesting that *sophrosune* refers to "the dominion of the *nous* [mind, intellect] over the lower impulses."[4] In Greek writings and tomb inscriptions this virtue is very often attributed to women and there "it always refers to a 'well-ordered life,' a life above all suspicion and criticism, an 'honest woman,' the opposite of dissoluteness. . . . The mores of such a woman are above reproach."[5]

It is this set of ideas that Paul seems to have in mind in his use of *sophrosune* in our passage. It appears that he means by it a *decency*[6] which is determined by self-control and good judgment and which expresses itself in personal deportment. In the Pastoral Epistles the word-family is especially used to indicate a conduct characterized by thoughtful self-control. The verbal form (*sophroneo*, "to be self-controlled") describes the conduct expected from young men (Tit 2:6),[7] and the adjective (*sophron*, "sensible;" "self-controlled") is used to designate a quality of church elders (1 Tim 3:2; Tit 1:8), older men (Tit 2:2) and young women (2:5). The source

---

[1]D. Zeller, "*Sophron* sensible; self-controlled," *Exegetical Dictionary of the NT*, vol. 3. p. 30.

[2]Spicq states that the different compounds of the verb *phroneo* "are, strictly speaking, untranslatable" (*Lexicon*, 3:359).

[3]Ibid.; cf. Ulrich Luck, "*Sophron*," *Theological Dictionary of the NT*, vol. 7, p. 1097.

[4]Cf. D. Zeller, "*Sophron*," *Exegetical Dictionary of the NT*, vol. 3, p. 330.

[5]Spicq, *Lexicon*, 3:365. Luck comments that as a feminine virtue *sophrosune* "is understood especially as the restraint and control of sexual desires; it does take the sense of chastity" ("*Sophron*," p. 1100). This meaning has been assigned to its usage in 1 Tim 2:9 by some commentators (e.g. Dibelius, *Pastoral*, p. 46). This suggestion seems to find extra support in the fact that the combination of *aidos* and *sophrosune* in Greek literature as female virtues express the ideas of reserve and control in sexual matters (David C. Verner, *The Household of God: The Social World of the Pastoral Epistles* [Chico, CA: Scholars, 1983], p. 168). This does not seem to be the only or even the primary concern of the apostle in 1 Tim 2:9. The context does not seem to allow for this only and exclusive meaning of the term.

[6]"Decency, chastity" have been suggested as the meaning of the word in our text by Arndt and Gingrich, *Lexicon*, p. 810; Zeller, "*Sophron*," p. 330, suggested "decency." This meaning, as we pointed out above, should not be limited only to sexual chastity.

[7]See Zeller, "*Sophron*," p. 330.

of this virtue is located in God's grace which teaches us all "to live sober [*sophronos*, "sensibly, in a disciplined fashion"], upright, and godly lives in this world" (2:11-12). In fact, Paul considers the active agent of this virtue to be the Spirit: "For God did not give us a spirit of timidity but a spirit of power and love and self-control [*sophronismos*, "self-discipline"]" (2 Tim 1:7). In a Christian setting this virtue is not the result of rational self-discipline but of the teachings of the gospel and of the work of the Spirit in the heart of all believers, both female and male.

Paul is requesting that the adornment of women be in the realm of "demeanor" (*katastole*), in the way they act and look; a demeanor qualified as "respectable/honorable" (*kosmios*), in other words, well-mannered and disciplined. He defines this adornment even more in terms of "modesty" (*aidos*), understood as avoiding excess and respecting the limits of propriety out of self-respect; and "decency" (*sophrosune*), a thoughtful self-control as defined by God's grace and the work of the Spirit in the life of the individual. These are the basic principles that are to govern the adornment of the believer.

2. Defining Improper Adornment

Paul proceeds to identify specific cases of personal adornment that are incompatible with the religious experience of the believer and with the instruction being given. Verse 9b is still governed by the combination of the main verbs used in 9a: "[*I desire women*] not [*to adorn themselves*] with braided hair or gold or pearls or costly attire." This negative command serves the purpose of clarifying in a more specific manner what the apostle had in mind on the subject of personal adornment.

The term *plegma* ("braided hair"), used only here in the NT, refers to "anything entwined, woven, braided," and not only to hair.[1] Nevertheless, it is accepted by scholars that in this particular case the reference is to braided hair. The fact that the term "hair" is not used in the text would suggest that in the context of adornment *plegma* was understood to refer to a hairdress of the same kind as the one mentioned and rejected by Peter. This particular hairdress is also considered by Paul to be incompatible with the true Christian spirit.

Here the term "gold" (*chrusion*), as we pointed out before, is most probably designating gold ornaments.[2] Some scholars have interpreted

---

[1]Bauer, *Lexicon*, p. 673; and Lindell and Scott, *Lexicon*, p. 1414.

[2]G. Schneider, "*Chrysos* gold," *Exegetical Dictionary of the NT*, vol. 3, p. 488.

this word in close connection with the previous, *plegma* ("braided hair"), to indicate that in the braiding of the hair gold adornments were used, that is to say the hair was at least plaited with gold.[1] This view, although possible, is exegetically very unlikely.[2] The most natural reading of the Greek is to take the conjunction "and" (*kai*) as introducing another item in the list. The other elements are placed in sequential relation to it by the use of the correlative particle "or."[3]

Paul also mentions "pearls" (*margaritais*) as a type of adornment that is to be rejected. These were considered to be very precious and used for the adornment of the body or the garments among the wealthy members of society.[4] The last item in the list is "costly attire" (*himatismo polutelei*). *Himatismos* was used in Greek to refer to clothing or apparel in general[5] and that explains why Paul qualified it by describing it as an expensive one. It has been pointed out that "in its various usages, this adjective means 'oppressively expensive' or 'rare and luxurious,' even 'sumptuous.'"[6] By using this term Paul is indicating that he is describing a type of apparel that is not simply expensive but *very* expensive. The emphasis is not necessarily on the costliness of the garment but particularly on a luxurious, ostentatious type of garment that does not reflect the nature of true beauty as understood by the Christian community.

---

[1]See Gordon Fee, *1 and 2 Timothy* (Peabody, Massachusetts: Hendrikson, 1984), p. 76. Based on that reading of the text it has been suggested that Paul was not forbidding the use of gold as ornament but the practice of braiding gold items into one's hair (John Temple Bristow, *What Paul Really Said About Women* [San Francisco, CA: Harper, 1988], p. 89).

[2]Attempts have been made to provide and exegetical basis for this suggestion arguing that "braided hair and gold" is a hendiadys, that is to say that both words together express one single idea: "hair plaited with gold." Cf. James B. Hurley, "Did Paul Require Veils or the Silence of Women? A Consideration of 1 Cor. 11:2-16 and 1 Cor. 14:3b-36," *Westminster Theological Journal* 35 (1973):199-200. In the New Testament this type of construction "serves to avoid a series of dependent genitives" (Blass, Debrunner and Funk, *Grammar*, p. 228), but in our passage this is unnecessary because what we have is a list of different items and not a series of genitives related in some way to the first one ("braided hair"). It could be argued that the next item, "pearls," could be related to "braided hair," e.g. braided hair adorned with pearls; but it is impossible to connect the last item, "costly attire," to "braided hair." The coordinating particles should be interpreted in the same way in all cases; as introducing different items.

[3]See R. Peppermuller, "*e* or; or else; than," *Exegetical Dictionary of the NT*, vol. 2, p. 111.

[4]See E. Plumacher, "*Margarite* pearl," *Exegetical Dictionary of the NT*, vol. 2, p. 385; and F. Hauck, "Margarites," *Theological Dictionary of the NT*, vol. 4, p. 472.

[5]See Bauer, *Lexicon*, p. 377.

[6]Spicq, *Lexicon*, 3:134.

3. Adornment and Spirituality

The apostle contrasts the exterior adornment he has just rejected with the one that should characterize Christian women. Once more the contrast is between "not" (*me*) that type of adornment "but" (*alla*) this other one. What is said in v.10 is related to what was said in 9a, and serves as a kind of a summary bringing the discussion to an end. It is now explicitly stated that there is a close connection between adornment and the spiritual experience of the individual; the one is a reflection of the other.

The adornment that the apostle is recommending is the one that corresponds to the religious claims of the believer: "As befits women who profess religion." The impersonal verb *prepo* ("be fitting") designates "that which is proper and appropriate"[1] but does not contain the idea of obligation in itself. In other words "what is fitting" is something that the persons addressed are not under compulsion to do. However, the usage of the word in the NT suggests that "righteousness and the exigencies of the situation make the conduct specified not only appropriate but imperative"[2] (cf. Matt 3:15; Eph 4:3; Tit 2;1; Heb 2;10; 7:26). Otherwise the basis for the expected conduct is discredited or disqualified. For instance, in our passage "what befits" is determined by a claim made by the women: they profess to be religious women. If they would not do that which befits the claim one could conclude that the claim may not be true.

The women Paul is addressing are described as persons who "profess religion." The verb *epanggellomai* ("profess") means among other things "to promise," "to profess" and "to lay claim to"[3] and in our passage expresses the idea of making a statement, declaring something. They claim *theosebeia* ("reverence to God," "religion"), to live a life pleasing to God.[4] Since this is the case it is expected from them to "substantiate this confession of their religion by good works."[5] The phrase "by [*dia*] good works" means

---

[1]Colin Brown, "*Prepo*, be fitting, seemly or suitable," *The New International Dictionary of NT Theology*, vol 2, p. 668.

[2]Ibid., p. 669.

[3]Arndt and Gingrich, *Lexicon*, p. 280; and J. Schniewind and G. Friedrich, "*Eppaggello*," *Theological Dictionary of the NT*, vol. 2, p. 576-78.

[4]The meaning of *theosebeia* "is as much moral as religious, connected with notions of purity, holiness, perfection, wisdom" (Spicq, *Lexicon*, vol. 2, p. 198.

[5]G. Bertram, "*Theosebes*," *Theological Dictionary of the NT*, vol. 3, p. 126.

"*by means of* good works" and is syntactically connected with the verb "to adorn themselves."[1]

In the Pastoral Epistles "good works" are considered to be a significant and indispensable sign of genuine Christianity.[2] Therefore, this type of work is also required from men (1 Tim 5:25) and more specifically from wealthy believers (6:18), from widows (5:10) and from all believers (Titus 3:8). The possibility of doing good works is based on the fact that Christ redeemed us from all iniquity (2:14), and that through the study of the Scriptures we are "equipped for every good work" (2 Tim 3:17). Hence, the adornment of good works is expected from those "who profess religion."

Paul brings his discussion on the proper adornment of women to an end on a positive description of the nature of true adornment. It is fundamentally living a life in which personal commitment to the Lord expresses itself through deeds that are a clear and visible manifestation of that commitment. The implication is that Christianity is so valuable and attractive that if it is put into practice it will beautify the lives of believers, making them honorable and respected people in the society in which they live.

C. Reason for and Purpose of the Instruction

We should now address the question of the reason for the discussion of the topic of female adornment in 1 Timothy. It has been suggested that Paul is reacting to the type of dress used by women who participated in the fertility cult of Artemis at Ephesus. His purpose would have been to instruct church members concerning the difference between Christian worship and pagan worship.[3] But there is no evidence in the immediate context or in the letter itself that would support that suggestion. As far as we can tell the adornment

---

[1]Spicq, *Pastorales*, p. 68; and Knight, *Pastoral*, p. 137.

[2]Dibelius and Conzelmann, *Pastoral*, p. 47; and J. Baumgarten, "*Agathos* good," *Exegetical Dictionary of the NT*, vol. 1, p. 7. The Greek for "good works" is *erga agatha* but we also find instead of *agathos* ("good") its synonym *kalos*. A comparison between 1 Tim 2:10 and 5:10 as well as Titus 1:16 and 2:7 will indicate that the two phrases are synonymous (see, J. Wanke, "*Kalos* beautiful; good," *Exegetical Dictionary of the NT*, vol. 2, p. 244).

[3]Sharon Hodgin Gritz, *Paul, Women Teachers, and the Mother Goddess at Ephesus: A Study of 1 Timothy 2:9-15 in the Light of the Religious and Cultural Milieu of the First Century* (Lanham, MD: University Press of America, 1991), p. 127.

rejected by Paul was very popular in his society and was not confined to the worship of Artemis.

It has also been suggested that the rejection of external adornment was an expression "of the woman's submission to her husband and a recognition of her place among men in general."[1] This would mean that Paul was in fact instructing women to demonstrate their submissiveness to their husbands through the way they dressed and adorned themselves. This idea is hardly present in our passage. In fact, there is no clear evidence to support the idea that in the Greco-Roman society the absence of exterior adornment was simply an expression of submission to the husband. The adornment Paul is rejecting was usually associated with ostentation and unchastity.[2]

A reading of the context of 1 Timothy 2:9-10 suggests that the improper adornment of some ladies may have been creating tensions in the church and damaging its reputation. In the previous verses Paul has shown concern about both elements. In 2:2 he appeals to believers to live a godly and respectful life in society. At the same time he exhorts them to worship in peace with each other (2:8). It is very probable that the type of dress worn by some ladies in church was not only ostentatious, but could have brought divisions in the church by establishing unnecessary social distinctions. At the same time the reputation of the ladies, and therefore of the church, was being

---

[1]David M. Scholer, "1 Timothy 2:9-15 and the Place of Women in the Church's Ministry," in *Women, Authority & the Bible*, Alvera Mickelsen, ed. (Downers Grove, IL: InterVarsity, 1986), p. 201; see also, *idem.*, "Women's Adornment: Some Historical and Hermeneutical Observations on the NT Passages," *Daughters of Sarah* 6 (January/February 1980): 3-6.

[2]Scholer, "Women's Adornment," has collected a series of statements from Jewish and Greco-Roman literature that according to him prove his point. A reading of those quotations indicate that expensive attire and the use of gold and precious stones was associated primarily with ostentatiousness and the moral value of the lady and not with her lack of submission to man. One of his examples may suffice; it is taken from two pseudonymous Neo-Pythagorean texts attributed to Phintys (second century BC): "A woman's greatest virtue is chastity. Because of this quality she is able to honor and cherish her own particular husband. . . . Accordingly a woman must learn about chastity . . . . I believe there are five qualifications [one of which is the cleanliness of the body]. . . . As far as cleanliness of the body is concerned . . . she should be dressed in white, natural, plain. Her clothes should not be transparent or ornate. . . . In this way she will avoid being overly dressed or luxurious or made-up. . . . She should not wear gold or emeralds at all—materialism and extravagance are characteristics of prostitutes. . . . She can ornament herself with modesty" (p. 4). See Thomas R. Schreiner, "An Interpretation of 1 Timothy 2:9-15: A Dialogue with Scholarship," in *Women in the Church: A Fresh Analysis of 1 Timothy 2:9-15*, Andreas J. Kostenberger, Thomas R. Schreiner, and H. Scott Baldwin, eds. (Grand Rapids, MI: Baker, 1995), p. 120, who comments concerning Scholer's evidence, "The devotion to and the honor of the husband demanded probably relate to faithfulness to the married bed than to submission." He adds, "Not a word is said about the lack of submission in 1 Timothy 2:9-10, and thus reading this theme into the text is questionable." However, even if the absence of jewelry was a sign of submission to the husband in the Greco-Roman culture, that is clearly not the main reason or the motivation for Paul's command.

damaged in the eyes of those in society who had high moral standards and who associated that type of adornment with questionable moral behavior.[1]

Paul, like Peter, seems to be very much interested in the reputation of Christianity among the non-Christians and its positive influence in society. In this respect Paul's advice corresponds quite well with what Peter had in mind. But while Peter's counsel was based primarily on the OT, in the case of Paul there is no reference to the Scriptures as he describes the nature of true Christian adornment. Hence, Paul seems to be closer to the language of the Greek and Roman moralists than Peter.

It is interesting to notice that the terminology used by him is very rare in the NT and in the LXX but common in Greek Hellenistic writings.[2] This could lead some to conclude that Paul is promoting Greco-Roman moral ideals in the Christian community. This is not necessarily wrong because he, as an apostle of the gospel and guided by the Spirit, would have been able to identify social practices that were compatible with the Christian message.[3] But the interesting thing is that for Paul the virtues he is promoting are also seen to be the result of the work of the Spirit and the grace of God in the life of the believer.[4] They are identified as or have become Christian virtues. One should take into consideration the probability that the apostle may have been basing his counsel on Old

---

[1]Cf. Keener, *Paul, Women*, p. 105; Schreiner, "Dialogue," p. 119; and Ben Witherington III, *Women in the Earliest Churches* (New York, NY: Cambridge, 1988), pp. 119-120, who comments, "The author is arguing not only for modesty and frugality in dress and worship, but also against the wearing of ostentatious or suggestive apparel or hairstyles that could attract the wrong sort of attention and compromise the moral witness of the church."

[2]We have in mind words like, *katastole* ("demeanor"), *kosmios* ("honorable"), *aidos* ("modesty"), and *sophrosune* ("decency").

[3]Ulrich Luck, discussing the use of the *sophron* family-group of words in the Pastorals, concludes, "The adoption of the group in the Pastorals should not be regarded as the intrusion of a Christian respectability originally alien to the gospel. Many motifs must be considered if one is to understand the acceptance of Greek and Hellenistic ethical traditions into primitive Christianity and the early Church. To the degree that faith is concerned with the life of the Christians in the world, the ethical traditions with their developed concepts help to ward off a pneumatic-ecstatic misunderstanding of faith. Also warded off are dualistic tendencies which, with ascetic or libertinistic consequences, might view life in the world as no longer life before God. Finally the waning of imminent expectation forced the Church to consider as concretely as possible the relation of Christians to the world in the spheres of life in which they were set" ("*Sophron*," p. 1103).

[4]This led D. Zeller to conclude that "even if the Pastorals adopt a Hellenistic ideal, they do allude to its salvation-historical relevance," and that Titus 2:12f. "shows that such self-control and reasonableness do not mean mere accommodation to one's civic environment, but are coupled rather with anticipation of the parousia" ("*Sophron*, p. 330). See also Schrage, *Ethics*, p. 258, who recognizes that "the Pastorals base their ethics on soteriology and interpret this ethics as a response to God's grace."

Testament traditions (e.g. Isa 3:16-23),[1] using language common to his readers. As in Peter we find here a congruence between Christian values and Hellenistic morality.

In the Greco-Roman world jewelry was also worn by men and moralists had instructions for them and not just for women.[2] One is forced to ask why Paul did not give similar instructions to men. This is difficult to answer but we pointed out that what Paul considers to be the true adornment of a Christian woman applies also to all members of the Christian community. It would be wrong to conclude that modesty in dress is required only from women but that men can dress immodestly; or that good works are not required from the male members of the church. He writes to women because in this particular case some of them are not living up to the Christian standard of personal deportment. Advice given to one segment of the Christian community does not mean that the rest of the community can do as they please. In fact in addressing one group Paul was instructing the church in general.[3]

D. Conclusion

Undoubtedly, Paul is defining some principles to be used by women when adorning themselves. This fact clearly suggests that Paul is not rejecting in *toto* exterior adornment for Christians.[4] Those principles set limits and at the same time open up tremendous possibilities for Christian

---

[1]Cf. Knight, *Pastoral*, p. 136, who suggested that Paul may be "applying to women Jesus' words in Mt. 5:28ff. and drawing on such OT passages as Is. 3:16ff."

[2]See Keener, *Paul, Women*, p. 104.

[3]See Keener, *Paul, Women*, p. 107: "Some women today may feel that it was unfair for Paul to pick on extravagantly dressed, well-to-do women but not on men; but Paul no doubt did so because they were the ones normally addressed by this particular issue in this congregation and more generally in antiquity. This does not mean, however, that Paul would not have addressed the same counsel to the men had they been creating a similar disturbance (difficult as this may have been in that culture). Paul would certainly not want men to dress in a manner that caused women to stumble, either. After all, 1 Timothy 2:8 tells only men to avoid wrath and disputing when they pray, but Paul hardly wanted women to pray in wrath and disputing!" One should not rule out the possibility that the way some of the ladies were adorning themselves was perhaps related in some way to the instructions being given by false teachers infiltrated into the church (see Dibelius and Conzelmann, *Pastoral*, p. 48; Fee, *1 and 2 Timothy*, p. 70; and Oden, *1 and 2 Timothy*, p. 95).

[4]It seems to me that Dibelius and Conzelmann went too far when stating that "the accent in the Pastorals lies not in the idea that women should (modestly!) adorn themselves, but rather that true ornamentation is not external at all" (*Pastoral*, p. 46; see also, Thomas D. Lea and Hayne P. Griffin, Jr., *1, 2 Timothy, Titus* [Nashville, TN: Broadman, 1992], p. 96). It is true that the main emphasis is on adornment that is interior and expresses itself through good deeds but, as we indicated already, in v. 9a the apostle shows that he is also interested in the proper demeanor (*katastole*) of women and that demeanor includes, but is not limited to, their external appearance.

witnessing. First adornment is to take place in the realm of the deportment or demeanor of women, in the way they act and dress. It should be honorable, inspiring respect for them as Christians ladies. Second, it should be modest, avoiding excess and respecting the limits of propriety out of self-respect. Third, it should be characterized by decency, a thoughtful self-control, influenced by God's grace and the work of the Spirit which expresses itself in good judgment.

The specific examples listed by Paul illustrate the type of adornment that would violate the principles enunciated by him. When it comes to hair dress there is a type that the apostle would consider appropriate for women but not the one he is describing. "Very expensive garments" implies that there is certain type of clothing that is compatible with Christian values. In other words, he is not rejecting proper care of the ladies' hair and the use of proper attire. However, in the case of jewelry he does not suggest or imply that some of it is modest. Paul simply says, "I do not desire women to adorn themselves . . . with gold ornaments and pearls." He could hardly have been more specific in rejecting the use of jewelry for personal adornment.[1]

The fact that Paul mentions only ornaments of gold and pearls have been taken by some to mean that he is rejecting only expensive jewelry.[2] According to this argument, Paul is only interested in the principle of economy. This line of reasoning may seem to find some support in the fact that he rejects "expensive clothes" (1 Tim 2:9), implying that inexpensive clothes are appropriate. However, this particular interpretation import into the text and idea that does not seem to be in Paul's mind and that sounds more like a rationalization than an exegetical conclusion. We base that criticism on several consideration.

First, the phrase "expensive clothes" does not emphasize the economical value of the clothes but, as already indicated, its ostentatious and luxurious nature. There is where the true emphasis is placed by Paul. The opposite type of dress that he is implicitly recommending is one that is not ostentatious and

---

[1]It has been argued that the language Paul is using is hyperbolic and that his real intent is located in the principles he enunciates, not on the specific examples he gives. What this would mean is that Paul's emphasis is on the effect of the adornment rather than on the items as such (Knight, *Pastorals*, p. 138). The specific examples are culturally determined. The conclusion drawn is that, "It is with braided hair, gold, pearls, and very costly garments as violations of this principle, not with hair however arranged or gold, pearls, or garments in and of themselves that he is concerned" (Ibid.). It appears to us that the specific cases or examples are inherently incompatible with the principles found in the text. Otherwise, they would not serve the purpose of illustrating the principle. Knight recognized that at least one of the items in the list of examples seems to be inherently inappropriate for the Christian: "The possible exception to this evaluation would be the qualifying word, *polutei*, 'very costly,' which carries a note of opprobrium because of its inherent inappropriateness" (ibid.).

[2]John T. Bristow, *What Paul Really Said About Women*, p. 90.

luxurious; he is not recommending one that is luxurious but less expensive. Second, the most probable reason why the apostle is distinguishing between different types of clothing is that clothing is a basic human need and it cannot be condemned *in toto*. However, wearing ornamental jewelry is not a basic human need that can and should be satisfied by wearing a less expensive type. Consequently, he does not make any explicit or implicit distinction between different types of jewelry. In other words there is no indication in the context that Paul is grading ornamental jewelry in terms of its cost in order to determine which one is or is not appropriate for personal adornment.

Third, Paul deals in the text with proper Christian adornment but he makes no room in his discussion for the use of inexpensive ornamental jewelry. Christian adornment is fundamentally interior, but expresses itself in the exterior presence and behavior of the believer. Again, had the issue being expensive jewelry, then the logical conclusion would be that ostentatious, yet inexpensive, ornamental jewelry is acceptable. There is nothing in the context to support the idea that Paul was encouraging the use of modest ornamental jewelry. Fourth, Paul mentions gold and pearls because they were the type of jewelry used in his days for personal ornamentation.[1] He does not include every item that would fall under that category, like precious stones and silver, indicating that the list was not exhaustive. He is clearly dealing with ornamental jewelry in any of its forms and the forms and materials used will vary from culture to culture.

Based on the examples Paul gives, we can conclude that he is rejecting adornment that has the simple purpose of establishing social distinctions in the church, perhaps separating the rich from the poor, and that are ostentatious, incompatible with the spirit of modesty and decency. Instead of that type of adornment he calls for good deeds which are an expression of the individual's commitment to God. Implicit is the idea that what we wear makes a statement about our values and the object of our true commitment. For those who fear the Lord ostentatious adornment should consist in the performance of good deeds on behalf of others.

---

[1]R. H. Higgins wrote, concerning jewelry in the Greek and Roman world, "Ancient jewelry was made chiefly of gold, silver and electrum (a natural alloy of gold and silver)" (*Greek and Roman Jewellery* [London: Methuen, 1961], pp. xli, xlii). Concerning precious and semi-precious stones he states, "Stones and similar natural objects served two principal purposes in ancient jewellery. (1) They were used in direct association with gold or silver as inlay, as ring-stones, or as beads or pendants attached to metal jewellery. (2) They formed independent articles of adornment, such as beads and pendants, finger-rings or bracelets. . . . In Greek and Roman times, . . . stones were used as much for their magical as for their decorative qualities. It appears that each stone had its own peculiar powers" (p. 37).

W O M E N   I N   T H E
P A S T O R A L   E P I S T L E S
1 TIM 2:11-15 AS PART OF THE CONTEXT OF 2:9,10

A. Introduction

In our previous discussion of 1 Tim 2:9,10 we made no attempt to relate the passage to verses 11-15, giving the impression that they were being ignored by us. Although it is true that the discussion on jewelry is a unit by itself, it is also true that the next few verses are still dealing with issues related to women in the church at Ephesus and therefore they deserve our attention in order to justify our exegetical procedure. The critical problem is as follows. If the passages on jewelry, as we have argued, are still normative for the church, are not the following verses that required women to be silent in church and not to teach, but to be submissive to men still normative? Why should one argue for one position and not for the other?

This is one of the problems that some evangelical theologians have confronted by considering 2:11-15 as normative but not 2:9,10.[1] Some have tried to deal with this problem suggesting that both passages are culturally determined;[2] while others have argued that we are only to retain the principles underlying the counsel given by the apostle.[3] They are at least attempting to be consistent in their interpretation of the whole passage.

Adventists have traditionally felt uncomfortable including in their hermeneutics the idea that some biblical passages could be culturally determined. Yet, we been willing to recognize that in certain situations that could be the case. The traditional example is the passage dealing with

---

[1]This inconsistency has been pointed out to them by, among others, Phillip B. Payne, "Libertarian Women in ephesus: A Response to Douglas J. Moo's Article, '! Timothy 2:11-15: Meaning and Significance,'" *Trinity Journal* 2 (1981):189; David M. Scholer, "1 Timothy 2:9-15 & the Place of Women in the Church's Ministry," *Women, Authority & the Bible*, edited by Alvera Mickelsen (Downers Grove, IL: InterVarsity, 1986), p. 202.

[2]Scholer, "1 Timothy 2:9-15," p. 202.

[3]E.g. Thomas R. Schreiner, "An Interpretation of 1 Timothy 2:9-15: A Dialogue with Scholarship," *Women in Church: A Fresh Analysis of 1 Timothy 2:9-15*, edited by Andreas J. Kostenberger, Thomas R. Schreiner, and H. Scott Baldwin (Grand Rapids, MI: Baker, 1995), pp. 118-19. However, his inconsistency shows when he says, "Perhaps we can preserve the principle of the command in verse 12 without denying women the right to teach men. After all, it was argued that the principle underlying verse 9,10 permits women to wear jewelry and clothing that is not seductive or ostentatious. However, the principle in verse 12 cannot be separated from the practice of teaching or exercising authority over men. There are some instances in which the principle and practice (e.g., polygamy and homosexuality) coalesce" (p. 140).

covering of the head of the women in worship recorded in 1 Cor 11:5-16. The *SDA Bible Commentary* says,

> . . . we may understand Paul, in 1 Cor 11:4-16, to be reasoning with the Corinthians as to the principle of propriety and religious decorum in terms of the particular customs of the day. Though ancient sources fail to give us unequivocal testimony as to custom in headdress in Corinth or elsewhere, it seems evident that custom have considered an uncovered head as proper for a man but improper for a woman. . . . Proceeding, then, on the reasonable assumption that Paul is here dealing with the application of a principle to the custom of the country and the times, we are able to take literally and meaningfully his words without following on to conclude that his specific application of the principle then, requires the same specific application today.[1]

Distinguishing between time-conditioned practices and what is permanently valid for the people of God across culture and time may not be as difficult as we think if we take into consideration that the Bible is its own interpreter. It is the witness of the Scripture in its totality that should be used to make a decision, keeping in mind that even in cases where local practices are being used there are always principles involved that are valid for us today. In the case of jewelry it appears to us that the abundant testimony of the Scriptures makes clear that in this particular case we are not dealing with an ancient cultural practice that is irrelevant for the church today. It was important in the Old and New Testaments, and it continues to be important for the people of God in our modern world.

I am not suggesting that 1 Tim 2:11-15 is describing a culturally determined practice and that, therefore whatever Paul is saying is of little or no value for the church. Undoubtedly, the interpretation of those verses is a difficult task and would require more space than we can afford here. Each

---

[1]*Seventh-day Adventist Bible Commentary*, vol. 6, edited by Francis D. Nichol (Hagerstown, MD: Review and Herald, 1957), p. 754. It also provides an example from the Old Testament: Moses was asked by the Lord to remove his shoes before him (Exod 3:5) because "It was evidently the custom in that area of the world–and it is, indeed, still the custom–to show respect for holy places by removing the shoes . . . . The principle of proper reverence still stands inviolate, but the method of expressing such reverence may vary greatly with countries and times." More recently Gerhard F. Hasel allowed for this interpretation: "While the 'head covering' itself may be related to the cultural custom of its time, the teaching on women praying and prophesying in church is in no way limited to Corinth, as Paul's theological argument based on Gen 1-2 indicates" ("Biblical Authority and Feminist Interpretation," *Adventists Affirm* 3 [Fall 1989]:17). C. Mervyn Maxwell is of the same opinion ("Let's Be Serious," *Adventists Affirm* 3 [Fall 1989]:30).

word in those verses has been carefully scrutinized by scholars because of the implications of the passage for the role of women in the church, more specifically their ordination to the gospel ministry. I must state from the beginning that this passage is not dealing with whether women should or should not be ordained, therefore I will not be dealing with that subject. In order to understand the passage correctly we must approach it from the perspective of the issues that Paul was confronting in the church at Ephesus as he describes them for us in the Pastoral Epistles. My approach is to identify what Paul is saying about women in the Pastoral Epistles and see how our particular verses fit into his overall concern. We will attempt to listen to the text itself.

B. Women in the Pastoral Epistles

The Pastoral Epistles contain a good amount of instructional materials addressed to women suggesting that they played a significant role in the church. Most of the material deals with their duties in their specific roles but in some cases the instruction sounds more like a reprimand, suggesting a situation of conflict in the church. Particular attention is given to the widows (1 Tim 5:3-16).

Timothy is counseled to give proper recognition to widows who are in need (5:3). Some of them are absolutely consecrated to the Lord (5:5), while others live for pleasure and are spiritually dead (5:6). Another problem occasioned by the number of widows in the church was that in some families the relatives were not providing for them and they had become a financial burden for the church (5:16). For such families Paul has very strong words: "If anyone does not provide for his relatives . . . he has denied the faith and is worse than an unbeliever" (5:8). This was a responsibility of the male and female members of the family (5:4, 16).

The church was to provide for widows who were in real need and who have been loyal members of the church (5:9,10). Young widows were not to be treated as widows because by providing for them they had free time to be idle and to go from house to house gossiping "saying things they ought not to" (5:13). Such conduct was creating serious problems in the church. Therefore it was better for them to get married (5:14).

Important instructions are given to a group of women who are either deaconesses or the wives of deacons. They are to be "women worthy of respect, not malicious talkers but temperate and trustworthy in everything" (1 Tim 2:11). Older women are called "to be reverent in the way they live, not to be slanderers or addicted to much wine, but to teach what is good" and to instruct younger women on family matters and religious piety (Titus 2:3-5).

Since female members were actively involved in the church it should not surprise us to discover that false teachers, who had infiltrated the church, would try to persuade them and use them in the promotion of their ideas. These false teachers were very much interested in "controversies and quarrels about words that result in envy, strife, malicious talk, evil suspicions and constant friction between men of corrupt mind, who have been robbed of the truth and who think that godliness is a means to financial gain" (1 Tim 6:3-5).

The attack of these false leaders was taken very seriously by Paul who decided to remind Timothy, Titus and the church elders the importance of preserving and teaching the true doctrine of the church (1 Tim 4:16; Titus 2:1; 1 Tim 5:17). Several times he calls it "sound doctrine" (1 Tim 1:10; 2 Tim 4:3; Tit 2:1), "good teaching" (1 Tim 4:6), "godly teaching" (1 Tim 6:3), and "my [Paul's] teachings." The Scriptures are the source of this reliable teaching (1 Tim 3:16). Over against this true doctrine Paul confronts the false teachings creeping into the church (1 Tim 6:1) and calls them "teachings of demons" (1 Tim 1:4). That strong emphasis on the teachings of the church as well as on the responsibility of the leaders to preserve *and teach* them is in the Pastoral Epistles a reaction to the work of the false teachers.[1]

Paul refers to the false teachers as those "who worm their way into homes and gain control over weak-willed women, who are loaded down with sins, and are swayed by all kinds of evil desires, always learning but never able to acknowledge the truth" (2 Tim 3:6-7). The verb *enduno*, translated "to worm in," means "to creep in" and suggests a deception that takes place by using false pretenses in order to have access to the victim.[2] These women were easy victims because they were loaded with their past sins and with evil desires and were willing to listen to those who may have something to offer to them. They were eager to learn from the false teachers but were unable to distinguish truth from error. The false teachers broke into their homes and captured them, gained control over them making them their instruments in the propagation of their false doctrines. Since some of these women were

---

[1]Rengstorf, "*Didaskalia*," *Theological Dictionary of the NT*, vol. 3, p. 162; H.-F Weiss, "*Didaskalia* teaching," *Exegetical Dictionary of the NT*, vol. 1, p. 317. It is worth pointing out that the word *didaskalia* ("doctrine, teaching") is used 21 times in the NT and 15 of those usages are found in the Pastoral Epistles.

[2]Cf. Guthrie, *Pastoral*, p. 170.

very wealthy they were more appealing to the false teachers who, because of their interest in financial gains, saw in them good financial contributors.

That description should not be interpreted to mean that only women were being deceived by the false teachers. The situation in the church seems to have been very serious and Titus is asked to "rebuke them [any one involved in it] sharply, so that they will be sound in the faith and will pay no attention to Jewish myths or to the commands of those who reject the truth" (Titus 1:14). Undoubtedly some men were also supporting the false teachers, but Paul addresses women because they may have been more effective or aggressive in propagating the heresy. It is that background, provided by the Pastoral Epistles themselves, that is indispensable for a proper understanding of 1 Tim 2:11-15.[1] The counsel given by Paul in that passage is his attempt to bring some order into the church by putting an end to the activity of the women who had been influenced by the views of the new teachers.

C. Analysis of 1 Tim 2:11-15
1. Learning in Silence - 2:11,12

The problem created by some women who brought the discussions and arguments of the false teacher to the church led Paul to say: "A woman should learn in quietness and full submission. I do not permit a woman to teach or to have authority over a man; she must be silent." There are some important details that we should notice in dealing with these verses.

First, the main interest of the passage is in principle a positive one—"women should learn."[2] In the context this learning experience seems to take place primarily in church. The women's thirst for knowledge is to be supplied by the church and not by the false teachers. The Christian church gave women the right to learn, together with the male members of the congregation.

---

[1]This is accepted by many scholars; e.g., Dibelieus and Conzelmann, *Pastoral Epistles*, p. 48; Payne, "Response," p. 185; Gordon D. Fee, *1 and 2 Timothy*, p. 70; Scholer, :1 Timothy 2:9-15, p. 203; Allan Padgerr, "Wealthy Women at Ephesus: 1 Tim 2:8-15 in Social Context," *Interpretation* 41 (1987):20-24; Stanley J. Grenz, *Women in the Church: A Biblical Theology of Women in Ministry* (Downers Grove, IL: InterVarsity, 1995), p. 127. Others reject that idea arguing that Paul is not addressing any local problem in Ephesus but giving general advise for women in the church; e.g., T. David Gordon, "A Certain Kind of Letter: The Genre of 1 Timothy," *Women in the Church: A Fresh Analysis of 1 Timothy 2:9-15*, edited by Andreas J. Kostenberger, Thomas R. Schreiner, and H. Scott Baldwin (Grand Rapids, MI: Baker, 1995), p. 60; Schreiner, "Dialogue," pp. 111-12.

[2]Schreiner, "Dialogue," p. 122, suggested that "the focus of the command is not on women learning, but the *manner* and *mode* of their learning." This is probably true but it does not alter the fact that Paul's approach is basically a positive one.

This does not seem to have been the case in the Jewish synagogue.[1] Therefore, according to Paul, the solution to the inroads that the false teachers were making among the women was not to forbid them to listen to the false teacher and then keep them in ignorance, but rather to develop their knowledge of the truth through teachers well trained in the gospel. This was a positive approach.

Second, in order for that learning to be effective Paul delineates a specific procedure: "Women should learn in silence." The meaning of the phrase "*in silence*" is of fundamental importance for the comprehension of the verse. The Greek text says *en hesuchia* indicating, through the use of the preposition *en* ("in"), that silence refers to the condition under which the learning experience takes place[2] and not to the permanent condition of women in church or in society. Extra biblical sources use this same phrase to designate the attitude expected from the person who wants to learn.[3] For instance, Philo of Alexandria writes, "Has someone said something worth hearing? Pay close attention, do not contradict them, be silent [*en hesuchia*]."[4] This is a nice definition of the phrase because it is placed in parallel with two other phrases that clarify its meaning. To learn in silence is to pay careful attention to the teacher and to avoid controversies and discussions with the instructor.

The term *hesuchia* ("quiet, tranquil") and words belonging to the same family, expresses in the New Testament the idea of silence as absence of conflict and not necessarily as absence of speech.[5] It is used to express at least three main ideas. (1) The silence that brings to an end or under control a discussion or confrontation (Acts 11:18; 21:14; 22:2); (2) keeping silence in order to avoid an open confrontation by using disruptive speech (Luke 14:4); (3) silence as a characteristic of the Christian life that consists of a life free from controversies that could disrupt the community of believers (1 Thess 4:11; 1 Tim 2:2).

---

[1]See for instance, Knight, *Pastoral Epistles*, p. 139.

[2]See among others, Thomas D. Lea and Hayne P. Griffin, Jr., *1, 2 Timothy, Titus*, p. 98; and Nancy J. Vyhmeister, "Church Behavior," p. 342.

[3]For examples consult, Keener, *Paul, Women*, p. 107.

[4]Philo, *Dreams* 2.264.

[5]See Angel Manuel Rodríguez, "Women's Words," *Adventist Review*, Nov 14, 1996, p. 27. Ben Witheringthon III, *Women in the Earliest Churches* (New York, NY: Cambridge, 1988), p. 120; and Spicq, "*Hesuchazo*," *Lexicon*, vol. 2, p. 178.

The use of the phrase "in silence" in the New Testament as well as outside it clearly indicates that Paul's request for quietness on the part of women "does not forbid questioning or speaking in general, but rather speaking that creates a disturbance."[1] The epistle itself suggests that the disruption was the result of the acceptance or of the influence of the false teachers. Paul is making clear that these women come to church not to teach but to learn the gospel truth and he is not willing to allow these ladies to disrupt the learning process. By forbidding this type of speech Paul is protecting the right of others to hear and learn; controversial speech is simply unacceptable.

Third, notice that the verse does not say to whom the woman is to be submitted,[2] thus forcing us to look at the context to understand the intention of the apostle when asking her to "learn *in all submission*," or "in complete submission."[3] Again, the use of the preposition *en* ("in") limits the submission to the context of the learning process helping us to interpret it either in terms of accepting the authority of the teacher[4] or accepting and submitting herself to the authority of the teaching itself.[5] In the first case the woman would have been asked not to contradict the authority of the teacher by arguing with him. The phrase would then be a synonym for "in quietness." In the second case Paul would be telling the woman that truth is found only in the instruction that she is receiving at church and not in the teachings of the false apostles and that therefore she is to submit to it, to surrender to it. Any

---

[1]C. H. Peisker, "*Hesuchia* rest, stillness, silence," *Exegetical Dictionary of the NT*, vol. 2, p. 125. Fee, *1 and 2 Timothy*, p. 72, has suggested that the expression be translated "in quiet demeanor," and rightly pointed out that this phrase is the key one in the passage because it is repeated at the end of verse 12. Those who argue the word means "in silence," that is to say not allowed to speak (e.g., Knight, *Pastoral Epistles*, p. 130; *Schreiner*, "Dialogue," p. 123), tend to ignore or de-emphasize the fact that Paul is describing what is expected in a learning process.

[2]For a list of the different suggestions made by scholars see, Schriner, "Dialogue," p. 124. Among others he mentions, God, the congregation, sound teaching, teachers, etc.

[3]R. Bergmeier, "*Hypotage* subjection, subordination; obedience," *Exegetical Dictionary of the NT*, vol. 3, p. 408. Examples of the use of "all" (*pas*) in the sense of "complete, full" see 1 Tim 4:9; 5:2.

[4]So, Padgett, "Wealthy Women," p. 24. Some have suggested that the submission of women mentioned in the text is their submission to their husband (see Richard M. Davidson, "Headship, Submission, and Equality in Scripture," in *Women in Ministry*, pp. 278-280, with bibliographical references); but see my comments below.

[5]Sharon Hodgin Gritz, *Paul, Women Teachers*, p. 130; Andrew C. Perriman, "What Eve Did, What Women Should Not Do: The Meaning of *Authenteo* in 1 Timothy 2:12," *Tyndale Bulletin* 44 (1993):131; and Vyhmeister, "Church Behavior," p. 342.

of those two possibilities make excellent sense in the context. However, it is probable that Paul has in mind both ideas at the same time. This suggestion can be supported by Gal 2:5 where Paul describes his confrontation with some false brothers to whom he did not yield "in subjection" for one moment. In other words, he did not recognize them as true teachers and neither did he submit to or accept their teachings.[1]

Fourth, because of the situation at the church in Ephesus Paul is not allowing women to teach. In other words, those who are students are not in a position to teach and even if they were to be permitted to teach the result would be controversy in the church because of the influence of the false teachers on these women.[2] The contrast with the previous verse is based on the fact that these women are not ready to teach,[3] therefore Paul says, "do not teach."[4] Besides, the prohibition against teaching is not universal or permanent because the New

---

[1]The same idea is expressed by the use of the verbal form in 1 Cor 14:22. To be in subjection to the prophets means to recognize them as prophets of the Lord and to accept their teachings. Witherington, *Women*, pp. 263-264, rightly comments, "What is being inculcated is a proper attitude and behavior in worship and not merely in relationship to men or husbands. The text says that they are to learn in all submissiveness, not that they are to submit to all men. It entails submission to the teaching and, by transference, to the one giving the faithful teaching whom one is to show respect for." Knight, *Pastoral*, p. 139, goes too far suggesting that the submission is to all men in authority in the church. Of course, respect for leaders of the church is something expected from male and female members of the church, but that is not what Paul is discussing here.

[2]See Donald Guthrie, *Pastoral Epistles*, p. 86; Fee, *1 and 2 Timothy*, p. 73; and Vyhmeister, "Church Behavior," p. 346.

[3]Less likely, but still possible, is the suggestion that the reason for not allowing women to teach was that they were teaching the heresies of the false teachers; cf., Payne, "Response," pp. 190-91. Perhaps both reasons are valid.

[4]We are not informed about the content of the teaching that is prohibited and neither are we told whether they were being forbidden to teach only men. Some have suggested that the women are only prohibited to teach men because that is the implicit object of the verb. The argument is that since "man" is the object of the next verb, authenteo, it is also the object of the verb "to teach" (see, Douglas J. Moo, "The Interpretation of 1 Timothy 2:11-15: A Rejoinder," *Trinity Journal* 2 (1981):201-202; Knight, *Pastoral*, p. 142). Payne, "Response," p. 175, has answered that argument indicating that the noun "man" is too far removed from the verb "to teach" and, therefore, it is only the object of the verb *authenteo* ("to have authority over"). In addition, we do not find in the New Testament examples of a grammatical construction in which two infinitives preceded by a finite verb has a single noun qualifying the two infinitives. Usually Acts 8:21 is quoted as an example but the grammatical construction is not the same as in 1 Tim 2:12 (contra Knight, *Pastoral*, p. 142)

Those who argue that Paul is prohibiting women to teach *men* modify what they argue Paul is saying by suggesting that the apostle is prohibiting them to teach men in the assembly or in church (e.g., Douglas J. Moo, "1 Timothy 2:11-15: Meaning and Significance," *Trinity Journal* 1 [1980]:65-67; Knight, *Pastoral*, p. 141). Moo himself recognizes that it is difficult to know what that would mean for the church today ("Rejoinder," p. 201). It seems to us that they are reading too much into the text.

Testament informs us that women could teach (e.g. Acts 18:26; Titus 2:4); in fact every church member is exhorted to teach (Col 3:16; 1 Cor 14:12).[1]

Fifth, the verb "to permit" ("I do not permit") seems to be used here to designate a limitation imposed on account of the situation at Ephesus and is not describing a universal one.[2] The phrase "I do not permit a woman" is followed by the use of two infinitives–to teach, to have authority–and then contrasted with what Paul expects from women–to be in silence.[3] We have seen that this last phrase is used by him to describe the conduct of women as students. There is no indicator in the context to the effect that the apostle is using this same phrase now in a different way. Therefore, the two things that Paul does not permit are to be defined in the context of a discussion of a woman's proper attitude as she is instructed in church. During the process of instruction she is not to assume the role of a teacher or "to have authority over a man."

Sixth, the meaning of the Greek term *authenteo* ("to have authority over") is uncertain but should be interpreted on the basis of its context. This is the only place in the New Testament were this verb is used, making it necessary for scholars to examine its usage in non-biblical

---

[1]See, Payne, "Response," pp. 173-74. The suggestion that the verb "to teach" designates here a particular teaching ministry to be exercised only and exclusively by men with ecclesiastical authority (so, Schreiner, "Dialogue," p. 128), is not suggested by the context. It is true that the Pastoral Epistles associate the verb "to teach" with Timothy (1 Tim 6:2) and church elders (1 Tim 2:2), but this does not mean that they are the only ones allowed to teach in church. The prophets were also God's instruments in building up the church (1 Cor 14:4; Acts 15:32). We must keep in mind that there were prophetesses in the apostolic church (Acts 21:9). The explicit instructions in this area in the Pastorals seems to be motivated by tensions created by the false teachers. In a situation where many people wanted to teach and where what was being taught by some was the opposite of the good doctrine it was necessary to identify those who will be the official instructors of the community.

[2]With Payne, "Response," pp. 170-71; Vyhmeister, "Church Behavior," p. 344; Witherington, *Women*, p. 120, suggests that the verb be translated "I am not permitting," to indicate that Paul is dealing with the situation in Ephesus. The verb *epitrepo* ("to permit") is used most of the time, if not always, in the New Testament to introduce local or temporally limited regulations (Witherington, *Women*, p. 120). Those who argue that the prohibition here is universal argue that it is the context that determines whether the prohibition is or is not universal (e.g., Moo, " Rejoinder," p. 199; Schreiner, "Diologue," pp. 1126-27). They believe that in this particular case it is universal because in verses 13,14 the apostle supports his arguments using the order of creation. But see our comments below.

[3]The grammatical structure is as follows: (1) a negated finite verb with a subject ("I do not permit a woman") + an infinitive ("to teach") + a coordinating conjunction (*oude*, "or") + another infinitive ("to have authority over") + the object of the second infinitive ("man") + the adversative *alla* ("but") + an infinitive ("to be [in silence]." For a discussion of it see, Kostenberger, "Sentence," pp. 82-84.

sources.[1] The most recent study of those sources have concluded that the verb is used in several different ways as indicated in the following table:[2]

The Meaning of *Authenteo*

1. To rule, to reign sovereignty
2. To control, to dominate
    a. to compel, to influence someone/thing
    b. middle voice: to be in effect, to have legal standing
    c. hyperbolically: to domineer/play the tyrant
    d. to grant authorization
3. To act independently
    a. to assume authority over
    b. to exercise one's own jurisdiction
    c. to flout the authority of
4. To be primarily responsible for or to instigate something
5. To commit a murder

Which one of those possible meanings did Paul have in mind? It is certainly not easy to decide but we can possibly rule out "to commit murder" because it does not fit the context and because this usage of the verb is attested in a document from the 10th century AD; and also "to rule" because this usage designates royal authority. It is obvious that the verb expresses the idea of authority. The following meanings are possible: to control, dominate, compel, influence, act independently, assume authority over, to domineer, and to flout the authority of. We have only the context to decide which one is more appropriate.

---

[1]Among the studies written on this verb see, Armin J. Panning, "Authenteo-A Word Study," *Winsconsin Lutheran Quarterly* 78 (1981):185-91; Carroll D. Osburn, "Authenteo (1 Timothy 2:12)," *Restoration Quarterly* 25 (1982):1-12; George W. Knight III, "*Authenteo* in Reference to Women in 1 Timothy 2.13," *New Testament Studies* 30 (1984):143-57; Catherine Clark Kroeger, "1 Timothy 2:12-A Classicist's View," *Women, Authority & the Bible*, edited by Alvera Mickelsen (Downers Grove, IL: InterVersity, 1986), pp.225-44; Leland Edward Wilshire, "The TLG and Further Reference to *Authenteo* in 1 Timothy 2.12," *New Testament Studies* 34 (1988):120-34; H. Scott Baldwin, "A Difficult Word: *Authenteo* in 1 Timothy 2:12," *Women in the Church: A Fresh Analysis of 1 Timothy 2:9-15*, edited by Andreas J. Kostenberger, Thomas R. Schreiner, and H. Scott Baldwin (Grand Rapids, MI: Baker, 1995), pp.65-80, 269-305.

[2]Taken from Baldwin, "Difficult Word," p. 73.

Whatever meaning we select we must keep in mind that Paul is dealing with the proper attitude of women as students. He already indicated he does not want them to assume the role of teachers and now he adds that they should not "have/assume authority over man." What does that mean? The different usages of the verb gives us several possibilities in the context of our passage: To try to control or dominate the teacher, to assume authority over him or even to flout his authority.[1] Any one of those would fit the context very well. Such an attitude on the part of women would disrupt the learning process creating serious conflict in the church. By assuming an attitude of authority that does not belong to them as learners these women would be acting independent of the rest of believers. In order to stop or avoid that situation Paul returns to his advice at the beginning of the passage: Let women "be/learn in silence."

Our discussion of 1 Tim 2:11,12 indicates that, in reaction to the work of the false teachers among the women of the church, Paul is motivating women to grow in the knowledge of the Christian faith. But this is to be done in a state of peace, free from discussions and divisive arguments, subjecting themselves to the Christian doctrine. Since they are not yet ready to be teachers Paul is not allowing them to teach and, in addition, he does not want them to misappropriate authority by acting independently of others in their search for knowledge.

---

[1]As noted in the chart the verb *authenteo* does not always have a negative meaning. We have selected the negative ones because the context is describing a type of behavior that is not acceptable to Paul when women are being instructed in church. Kostenberger, "Complex Sentence," has studied the syntactical parallels to 1 Tim 2:12 in the New Testament and in extra-biblical literature and conclude that the verb *authenteo* is used in that passage in a positive way. Two activities are prohibited in 2:12-to teach and to have authority over. This is what he concluded in his study of the parallel passages: They "can be grouped into two patterns of the usage of *oude* ["or"]: Pattern # 1: two activities or concepts are viewed positively in and of themselves, but their exercise is prohibited or their existence denied due to circumstances or conditions adduced in the context. Pattern # 2: Two activities or concepts are viewed negatively and consequently their exercise is prohibited or their existence denied or to be avoided. In both patterns, the conjunction *oude* coordinates activities of the same order, that is, activities that are either both viewed positively or negatively by the writer or speaker" (p. 85). He then applies this rigid rule to our passage and concludes that since "to teach" is a positive activity in and of itself-although prohibited under certain circumstances-the verb "to have authority over" is also to be taken in a positive sense (the legal right to have authority and not in the sense of to control, to flout someone's authority).

I examined the parallels that Kostenberger found and discovered that there is a third pattern: Pattern # 3: One activity or concept is viewed positively in and by itself while the other is viewed negatively, but the exercise of both of them is prohibited due to circumstances or conditions adduced in the context. This is the pattern emerging from Matt 12:19 and possibly 2 Thess 3:7,8. This is very close to what we have in 1 Tim 2:12: to teach is positive in and by itself; to assume authority, to flout the authority of someone is viewed negatively, but the exercise of both of them is prohibited due to circumstances adduced in the context. But even if Kostenberger is right, his first pattern allows for the verb "to have authority over" to be taken in a negative way. According to him it is the context that determines the reason why the two activities are prohibited. In our passage the reasons are that these women are not yet qualified to teach (they are still learning) and that they are trying to control the person who is teaching them.

2. Adam and Eve - 2:13,14

The last three verses in the passage that we are studying are very difficult to interpret, particularly verse 15. Let us deal first with verses 13 and 14: "For Adam was formed first, then Eve. And Adam was not the one deceived; it was the woman who was deceived and became a sinner."

We should observe the importance of the introductory word "for" (Gk. *gar*). What is its function in this sentence? The possibilities are essentially two: to take it as providing a reason for what was said before[1] or an explanation of what was said before using an illustration.[2] Those who opt for the first interpretation argue that Paul is giving reasons for the prohibitions against teaching and having authority over men introduced in the previous verse. They find two reasons for the subordination of women to man. The first one is the order of creation: Adam was created first and then Eve, therefore women are to be in submission to men (probably the husband). The second is that women are easier to deceive than man and cannot be entrusted with apostolic teachings.[3]

That interpretation presupposes that the main concern of the previous verses is the recognition on the part of women that they are to be under the authority of men. But as we have indicated that is not the case. The main interest of the apostle is regulating the attitude expected from women as they are instructed in church. Paul is trying to control the influence of the false teachers as they work through some of the women. He wants women and men to work together against a common threat. Now in verse 13 he illustrates what he just stated in the previous verses. The verse contains a simple biblical fact: Adam was created first and then Eve. This is the way God created the human race. There is no suggestion here that because Eve was formed after Adam she was in some way inferior or subordinated to him.[4] In fact that idea is also absent from the creation account in Genesis. In this particular case the chronological order should not "be regarded as significant since Adam was created after the animals and was nevertheless given dominion over them. The point here is that mankind

---

[1]E.g., Moo, "1 Timothy 2:9-15," p. 68; Knight, *Pastoral*, p. 142; Schreiner, "Dialogue," p. 134.

[2]E.g., Payne, "Response," p. 176; Witherington, *Women*, p. 122; and Vyhmeister, "Church Behavior," pp. 346-47.

[3]E.g., Moo, "1Timothy 2:9-15," p. 71; Schreiner, "Dialogue," p. 146. Gordon, "Certain," p. 61, comments that "Paul's instruction is grounded not in what was happening in Ephesus but in the created and fallen order."

[4]The idea that here Paul is using the creation account to demonstrate that Eve was under the authority of Adam is supported by a number of scholars; see e.g., Moo, "1 Tim 2:915," p. 68.

consisted of a pair (Adam and Eve). Eve was intended as a companion to Adam. Their relationship is not to be considered as competitive but as complementary."[1] Paul is using the creation account to illustrate the importance for men and women to remain and work together as they confront deception.

Paul goes on to add that in spite of the fact that they were created to be together Eve, not Adam, decided to act independently and as a result she was deceived. He puts the emphasis on the action of Eve and its damaging consequences because his advice is directed to ladies. It is important to notice that in this passage the sin of Eve did not consist in her rebellion against her supposed subjection to the authority of Adam but rather in listening and falling into deception.[2] She, like the women in the church at Ephesus, was searching by herself for knowledge but was deceived and found herself in transgression. She was persuaded by an outsider to believe something that was not true.[3] This illustrated quite well the situation in the church at Ephesus where some women, Paul says, "have in fact turned away to follow Satan" (1 Tim 5:15). Perhaps, implicit is also the idea that once she was deceived Eve became also an instrument of deception for others.

3. Childbearing - 2:15

The final verse begins with the verb "to save" in the passive future tense, third person singular–"She will be saved"–, shifting in the following verb to the third personal plural–"If they continue in faith, . . ." The natural way of reading the verse would suggest that the first verb is still referring to Eve but the plural in the second verb indicates that the apostle has in mind the women to whom he is writing. One could conclude that for Paul the experience of Eve illustrates the experience of some women and this allows him to move from the singular to the plural.[4]

The next difficulty is located in the meaning of the phrase "[she will be saved] through childbearing [*teknogonias*]." This appears at first to be a

---

[1]Donald Guthrie, *The Pastoral Epistles*, p. 87. Witherington, *Women*, p. 123, suggest s that the fact that the passage states that Adam and Eve were"both formed by God in like manner" suggests their equality; also Payne, "Response," p. 189.

[2]It must be pointed out that the issue in verse 14 is not that women should not teach but on the threat of being deceived by listening to false teachers. The illustration from the creation account emphasizes that fact. See Fee, *1 and 2 Timothy*, p. 74; cf. Gordon, "Certain," p. 62.

[3]See, Perriman, "Eve," p. 139.

[4]Cf. Scholer, "1 Timothy 2:9-15," p. 196; and Vyhmeister, "Church Behavior," p. 348.

strange idea and consequently has resulted in different interpretations.[1] The basic questions have to do with the meaning of the verb "will be saved" and the noun "childbearing." The verb has been interpreted by some as meaning salvation in a spiritual sense or as salvation in the sense of physical preservation.[2] There are two common interpretations of the passage, the first being that the woman who fell in sin, Eve, will be saved by "bearing a child," the Messiah. That is to say, women too are objects of God's grace. The second is that the passage is stating that the role of women is to have children and to remain in the faith. During childbearing they will be protected or preserved by God.

Both interpretations face difficulties. The term "childbearing" is a strange way of referring to the Messiah because the term describes the act of giving birth to a child and not to the child that was born. On the other hand if the text is referring to the women's ability of childbearing then Paul would be saying that for a woman salvation is the result of bearing children. That would be theologically unsound. Besides, the verb "to save" in the Pastoral Epistles designates God's work of preserving humans from eternal death[3] and not from the danger of death during childbearing.

What, then, can we say? Very little. The second part of the verse seems to express the main interest of the apostle: "If they continue in faith, love and holiness with propriety." In its context verse 15 is a call to women to remain in the faith and to live a holy life. This is an invitation to preserve their commitment to the Christian gospel by not listening to the false teachers. In that case the first part of the passage could be referring to the salvation available to them through the Child born of a women and promised to Adam and Eve. In spite of its difficulties, this seems to be the only

---

[1]For a discussion of the different interpretations see, Moo, "1 Tim 2:9-15," p. 71; Fee, 1 and 2 Timothy, p. 75; Grenz, *Women*, pp.138-40; Knight, *Pastoral*, pp. 144-49.

[2]This summary was taken from Knight, *Pastoral*, pp. 144-45.

[3]See for instance, Fee, *1 and 2 Timothy*, p. 75, who comments that if the phrase means "to be kept safe through childbirth" then the promise is not true to reality because many godly Christian women died in childbirth. He adds, "Paul's use of the word saved throughout these letters disallows it (he always means redemption, from sin and for eternal life, as in 1:15-16 and 2:4)." Andreas J. Kostenberger suggested that the verse be translated: "She (i.e., the woman) escapes (or is preserved; gnomic future) [from Satan] by way of procreation (i.e., having a family)" ("Ascertaining Women's God's-Ordained Roles: An Interpretation of 1 Timothy 2:15," *Bulletin for Biblical Research* 7 [1997]:142). The fact that he has to insert into the text the phrase "from Satan" rests credibility to his suggestion. Besides, if Paul's intention was to express the idea of preservation ("escape") he could have used *rhyomai* ("save, rescue, deliver") used by him in other places (e.g., 2 Tim 3:11; 4:17, 18), and not a verb that he consistently used to designate eternal salvation.

interpretation that brings the passage into clear theological harmony with the doctrine of salvation.[1] Salvation is available to all, including women, but they have to remain loyal to the faith entrusted to them, that is to say, they should not pay attention to false teachings.

D. Conclusion

The passage we have studied is difficult to interpret and that should make us very sensitive to the importance of taking into consideration the context that the apostle himself provides for us. If we look at that context it becomes clear that Paul is dealing with a particular situation that arose in the church in Ephesus. He was giving specific instructions on how to control or even to bring to an end the work of the false teachers in that church, particularly among some of the female members of the congregation. There is practically nothing in his counsel that we cannot implement today in a church that may be facing the same or similar conditions as those found in the church in Ephesus. His advice can be equally applied to men and women who, under the influence of false teachings, create tensions and disruptions in our churches. Yes, Paul was addressing a specific situation but in doing so he was also instructing us.

---

[1]Knight, *Pastoral*, p. 147, comments, "That through which, or by means of which, the women will be saved is *teknogonia* (a biblical hapax), 'bearing a child.' Although it is not certain that the definite article is to be stressed . . . if it is, then the noun plus the article would refer to '*the* bearing of a child'; but even without such a stress the reference to 'bearing a child' could well stand for the birth of the promised seed of the woman."

SUMMARY OF THE BIBLICAL MATERIALS
A FOUNDATION FOR THE STANDARD OF THE CHURCH

Having gone through the biblical passages dealing with the subject of jewelry it is now time to summarize our findings and reflect on them. In the next two chapters we will attempt to clarify their significance and implications for the church and the individual believer. In the process we will have the opportunity to deal with some of the specific questions being asked with respect to the church's standard on jewelry. The need for this type of discussion and analysis has already been demonstrated in the first chapter of this document.

A. Summary of the Biblical Teaching on Ornamental Jewelry

As we look back to the results of our biblical inquiry into the subject of jewelry there are a number of things that could be said as we try to summarize the major concepts associated with it. This will provide for us the basis for the discussion on the meaning and implications of those concepts for the church today.

1. Diversity of Functions

The biblical evidence indicates that jewelry was used and owned for multiple reasons and purposes that in many cases were complementary and not necessarily mutually exclusive. We consider this to be a significant piece of evidence in our attempt to understand the biblical attitude toward jewelry because it forces us to reconsider the idea that in general the primary purpose of jewelry is personal ornamentation. Its ornamental function is not to be denied, but its primary function lies elsewhere. The beauty of the ornaments becomes a vehicle to achieve a more narrow and, from the point of view of the wearer, a more meaningful or important purpose; for instance, impress others with personal wealth, social position and power, or religious function.

2. General Pejorative Attitude

The biblical evidence clearly demonstrates that overall there is a pejorative attitude toward jewelry in the Scriptures. We find God Himself asking His people to remove the ornaments from their bodies in the context of a call to re-commitment to the Lord (Exod 33:5,6; cf. Gen 35:2-4). This is also indicated by the prophetic indictment against almost all types of jewelry worn by both men and women (Isa 3:18-21). The fact that the Israelites removed their ornaments from Sinai onward suggests that early Israelites did not wear jewelry. The archaeological evidence indicates that such may have been the case because, with rare exceptions, excavations in early Israelite sites have uncovered very little jewelry and only of a poor quality.

This tendency to devaluate jewelry is reflected in the fact that no mention is made of it in cases and situations where we would expect reference to its use. Thus, for instance, during the creation of Adam and Eve, and particularly after the Lord dressed them (Gen 3:21), there is no explicit or implicit reference to ornaments. In Rev 12:1,2 a woman is used as a symbol of God's people but there is a total absence of jewelry on her body. Yet, the woman representing the enemies of God's people is described as loaded with jewelry (Rev 17:4). Moreover, in total discontinuity with ancient Near Eastern practices, the God of Israel wears no jewelry. He never appears using ornaments and He is never seen in vision by the prophets wearing them. Once it is acknowledged that there is a significant number of passages in the Bible dealing with jewelry, it would be incorrect to attribute this situation to mere chance. It does reflect the attitude of the biblical faith toward jewelry and suggests that in general it was not positive.

3. Not Intrinsically Evil

One should also accept the fact that the Bible does not consider jewelry to be essentially evil. Otherwise it would have been impossible for God to order Moses to make a dress for Aaron adorned with jewelry, or for the king to wear a crown, or for anyone to have a signet ring. But all of those cases are to some extent appropriate usages of jewelry. Jewelry cannot be essentially evil because the beautiful materials used in its production were created by God Himself. Moreover, minerals are not moral agents but humans are. The evil of jewelry is to be located in the heart of the wearer and not simply in the object itself.

4. Restricted Usage of Jewelry

If we are willing to accept that in the Bible jewelry has different functions, that there is a general pejorative attitude toward it, and that, nevertheless, it is not intrinsically evil, then we must also accept that not all of its usages are approved by the Lord. The Bible does have a restrictive attitude toward the use of jewelry. Here we must take care to distinguish what is acceptable from what is not. The fact is that most usages of jewelry are rejected by the biblical writers.

Religious, magical, and protective jewelry is probably rejected because of idolatry. More important is the fact that no religious jewelry was prescribed for the Israelites through which they could express their religious convictions and their commitment to the Lord. This is not an argument based on the silence of the biblical record. The Lord, as we have demonstrated, told the Israelites what to wear in order to inform others that they worshiped Him alone and no other gods. He required from them a particular symbolic attachment on their clothes, but it was not jewelry. This symbol indicated that they were holy to the Lord (Num 15:37-41). According to the New Testament such a holy life should adorn the Christian (1 Pet 3:4,5).

The use of jewelry as symbolizing social status, power and authority is restricted only to a few cases. Here we can mention the dress of the high priest, the jewelry of the king and the queen, and the signet ring. Of those, only the first was explicitly instituted by God Himself and the others seem to have been permitted or tolerated by Him. In these cases the element of adornment plays a secondary role. When others besides the royal couple used jewelry to establish social distinctions the prophets raised their voices against them (Isa 3:18-21; 1 Tim 2:9,10; 1 Pet 3:3-6), indicating this type of jewelry was not fully acceptable. But those exceptions serve to show that, at least in some cases, functional jewelry was accepted.

5. Ornamental Jewelry Is Rejected

The Scriptures are clear that ornamental jewelry was not to be part of the personal adornment of the people of God. Although jewelry enhanced the appearance of the individual, it was worn for another reason. The jewelry used by the high priest beautified him, but its primary purpose was to identify him as the leading spiritual figure in Israel and representative of the people before the Lord. Whenever the functional nature of a piece of jewelry was rejected, its ornamental function was also rejected. In other words there is no evidence to indicate that, for instance, magical jewelry was acceptable if used only for ornamental purposes. Rejection of the one was also rejection of the other.

In New Testament times jewelry was commonly used for personal adornment, but even there other functions were associated with it also. In cases where jewelry was primarily ornamental the biblical passages are clear in rejecting it and in describing the nature of true personal adornment as the enactment of Christian virtues in the daily life of the believer (1 Tim 2:9,10; 1 Pet 3:3-6). To be sure, personal adornment is not totally rejected, but a particular type of exterior adornment is identified as incompatible with the Christian life. Ornamental jewelry falls into this category of adornment.

We can summarize our discussion by saying that the Bible rejects the use of ornamental jewelry by God's people while at the same time accepting or tolerating a restrictive use of some functional jewelry. It is obvious that the issue of jewelry in the Bible cannot be dealt with in terms of categories of totally wrong or totally right. On this basis, the church must abide by what is clear and use biblical principles to deal with those areas where a personal decision is required.

B. Foundation of the Adventist Standard on Jewelry

Our study has shown that there is significant material on the subject of jewelry in the Bible, distributed from Genesis through Revelation. The subject is well attested in the Scriptures and of concern for biblical writers. This phenomenon should limit significantly the argument that the Adventist standard on ornamental jewelry stems from the Victorian age during the 1800s. The fundamental reason why the Adventist church established this standard was because our pioneers believed that it was a biblical teaching, one they inherited from other Christian communities.

A Christian standard on jewelry existed long before there was an Adventist or a Protestant. It appears in the time of the early post-apostolic church, to say nothing of the apostolic church, where it was supported not simply on the basis of cultural concerns but on the basis of the Scriptures.[1] It is a fact that during the first three centuries of the Christian era the church held to a very high standard on the use of ornamental jewelry. Tertullian (160-225 AD) wrote against ornaments consisting of gold, silver, and gems but indicated at the same time that he was not encouraging disregard for good personal appearance. He pointed to "the limit and norm and just measure of cultivation of the person. There must be no overstepping of the line to which simple and sufficient refinement limit their desires–the line that is pleasing to the Lord."[2] Obviously he had in

---

[1]Excellent material on this subject is cited in Bacchiocchi, *Christian Dress*, pp. 74-100.

[2]Tertullian, *On the Apparel of Women*, I.4; II.5, in *Ante-Nicene Fathers*, vol. 4, edited by Alexander Roberts and James Donaldson (Grand Rapids, MI: Eerdmans, 1979), p. 16, 20.

mind 1 Pet 3:3,4 and 1 Tim 2:9,10, which he quoted in other places where he discussed proper Christian adornment.[1]

We also find Clement of Alexandria condemning ornamental jewelry, challenging women to "utterly cast off" ornaments[2] and telling men that there is no need for them to wear ornaments of gold.[3] Earrings are rejected because "the Word prohibits us from doing violence to nature by boring the lobes of the ears."[4] Interestingly, Clement makes a distinction between ornamental jewelry and functional jewelry. He argues that the Word permits a man or a woman to wear a finger-ring of gold "for sealing things which are worth keeping safe in the house."[5] But he goes further by suggesting that women married to men who are not Christians and who want them to wear ornamental jewelry should do it only to please their husbands. But it should be their goal gently to draw their husbands to simplicity.[6]

During the third century one can begin to detect a small tendency to relax the standard on jewelry. However, it was still defended by writers such as Cyprian, Bishop of Carthage (d. 258), who admonished wealthy women who wanted to use their wealth as they pleased, to "use them, certainly, but for the things of salvation; use them, but for good purposes; use them, but for those things which God has commanded, and which the Lord has set forth. Let the poor feel that you are wealthy; let the needy feel that you are rich."[7] Then he quoted Paul, Peter and Isaiah to demonstrate that those who adorn themselves with gold, pearls, and necklaces "have lost the ornaments of the heart and the spirit."[8] Cyprian associated jewelry with moral corruption (prostitution) and immodesty.

By the fourth century jewelry was becoming common in the church, leading John Chrysostom (c. 347-407 AD) to address the issue in some of

---

[1]Tertullian, *De corona* 14, in *Ante-Nicene Fathers*, vol. 3, p. 102.

[2]Clement of Alexandria, *The Instructor* II.13, in *Ante-Nicene Fathers*, vol. 2, p. 268.

[3]Ibid., III.1, (p. 271).

[4]Ibid., III.11, (p. 285).

[5]Ibid. The seal was expected to have some Christian emblem engraved on it. See F. L. Cross, editor, *The Oxford Dictionary of the Christian Church* (London: Oxford University Press, 1958), p. 1167.

[6]Ibid.

[7]Cyprian, *Treatise II: On the Dress of the Virgins* 11, in *Ante-Nicene Fathers*, vol. 5, p. 433.

[8]Ibid., 13, p. 433.

his homilies. He considered ornaments of gold unnecessary for men and women. In fact, it was ridiculous, he said, for a woman to come to church wearing her gold ornaments: "For what possible reason does she come in here wearing golden ornaments, she who ought to come in that she may hear [the precept] 'that they adorn not themselves with gold, nor pearls nor costly attire'? (1 Tim. ii. 9.) With what object then, O woman, dost thou come? Is it indeed to fight with Paul, and show that even if he repeat these things ten thousand times thou regardest them not? Or is it as wishing to put us your teachers to shame as discoursing on these subjects in vain?"[1] Chrysostom concludes this section with a very specific appeal: "Let not the image of God be decked out with these things: let the gentlewomen be adorned with gentility, and gentility is the absence of pride, and of boastful display."[2]

I have given special attention to these early Christian writers because they illustrate the initial Christian understanding of the biblical view on ornamental jewelry, long before the Victorian Age. The early centuries are marked by strong resistance to the use of ornamental jewelry by believers. After the fifth century, as Bacchiocchi has pointed out, jewelry became the official adornment of the clerical orders and during the remainder of the Middle Ages was very popular among Christians.[3] The Reformers condemned this practice of the church and called Christians back to a life of simplicity, discouraging the use of jewelry for personal adornment. This was particularly the case among the Anabaptists who sought to reform the church not only in terms of doctrines but also in biblical life style. This tradition was continued among the Mennonites, Brethren, and Methodists, among others.[4]

Adventists are inheritors of this genuine biblical, early catholic, and protestant understanding of personal ornamentation. History indicates a recurring tendency among those who have upheld the high biblical standard on ornamental jewelry to relax the standard until it is virtually non-existent. Perhaps the reason is that its biblical basis is forgotten or

---

[1]John Chrysostom, *Homilies on Hebrews* XXVII.13, in *Nicene and Post-Nicene Fathers*, vol. 14, edited by Philip Schaff (Grand Rapids, MI: Eerdmans,1978), p. 497.

[2]Ibid. See also his *Homilies on Timothy* VIII, in *Nicene and Post-Nicene Fathers*, vol. 13, pp. 433, 434.

[3]Bacchiocchi, *Christian Adornment*, pp. 83-86.

[4]Ibid., pp. 83-94.

considered irrelevant. This is the kind of pressure the Adventist church faces today.

C. Conclusion

The multiplicity of biblical references to jewelry, when carefully analyzed, reveals a consistent pattern of meaning and coherence throughout the Scriptures. By recognizing that in the Bible jewelry has different functions and that some of them are accepted or tolerated while others are rejected we are able to understand the attitude of the biblical writers toward jewelry. It was precisely that biblical material that provided to the Christian church, and more particularly to the Adventist church, the very foundation for a biblical standard on jewelry.

Implications for the Church and Potential Dangers

IX

Those who believe that the Bible is their norm of faith and practice are willing to raise the question of how the biblical teachings on jewelry affect their Christian life. We recognize that it is a sensitive matter to guide people regarding what to wear or not to wear, but the fundamental question in this case becomes that of the authority of the Bible in our lives. Adventists always have claimed to be willing to listen and submit to the will of God as expressed in the Scriptures, and for that reason we should feel free to explore the implications of the biblical teaching on jewelry for us today. Interestingly, this issue is not as complex as some tend to believe once we understand the biblical view on this subject. Hence, let us explore some of the implications.

A. Some Implications
1. Adventist Standard on Jewelry and the Bible
The Adventist standard on jewelry rejects ornamental jewelry while at the same time recognizing that there is such a thing as functional jewelry and that using it is not necessarily a violation of the standard. As discussed previously, this is what the Bible states with respect to the use of jewelry. It is true that for some people it is difficult to accept the concept that jewelry could have today different functions, but jewelry even in the Western World does fulfill several functions. Religious jewelry is common in the New Age movement as well as among some Christians (e.g. the Crucifix, among Catholics); and interest in the occult has brought with it the use of protective jewelry. In some countries jewelry is used to indicate the social role of queens, kings, and tribal chiefs. Of course, the most well known piece of functional jewelry is the wedding band, used as a symbol of loving commitment to the spouse. However, in most cases the primary function of jewelry today seems to be ornamental. It is this ornamental aspect that the church, following the Scriptures, has rejected as inappropriate for Christians.

Ornamental jewelry usually, but not exclusively, takes the form of earrings, nose rings, bracelets, rings, necklaces, and anklets worn to enhance the appearance of the individual. To some extent this is the implicit definition of ornamental jewelry that we find in the "Action on Display and Adornment" taken during the 1972 Annual Council of the General Conference. It stated: "That in the area of personal adornment necklaces, earrings, bracelets, jewelled and other ornamental rings should not be worn."[1]

2. Restrictive Use of Functional Jewelry

Without doubt this is the area that tends to create confusion in the mind of some Adventists who would rather reject all jewelry as evil, or among those who are interested in rejecting the standard while preserving the principles behind it. In allowing a limited use of functional jewelry the church is following the biblical position. The question that the church confronts here is defining functional jewelry and stating at what point it becomes ornamental jewelry.

Since most societies seem to be have a clear cultural understanding of what functional jewelry is it is not necessarily difficult to identify it. Perhaps what one needs to ask is, What is the particular purpose of this piece of jewelry in our particular culture? If one is unable to find a purpose then it is probably ornamental. In the western world functional jewelry is usually easy to identify because its function is an intrinsic part of its marketing possibilities and satisfies a particular need in the attire or life of the individual. For instance, a watch is made with the express purpose of helping us to keep track of time; a wedding ring is sold precisely as a wedding ring; and cufflinks are made in such a way as to facilitate holding cuffs together. The brooch may still be a functional ornament if it hold together pieces of clothing, as toggle pins did in the ancient world.

Obviously, functional jewelry could be made in such a way that its ornamental function outshines any other useful purpose. In that case it must be considered inappropriate for a Christian to use it. On what basis is one to decide on this issue? The solution that the biblical text seems to suggest is to use biblical principles to determine what is and is not appropriate for personal adornment. Probably one could identify many principles, but the church has identified the three most important ones: simplicity, modesty, and economy. Functional jewelry should be evaluated on the basis of these three principles.

"*Simplicity*," although not a common biblical term, is considered to be an important Christian virtue. In the New Testament the Greek term *haplotes*

---

[1]See Appendix I.

seems to be the most important one used to express concepts of simplicity, singleness, sincerity.[1] The utilization of this term in the Greek translation of the Old Testament and in the New Testament indicates that simplicity consists of an undivided commitment to a single purpose, i.e., the service of God. It is characterized by the absence of ambiguous behavior or duplicity (cf. 2 Cor 11:3; Matt 6:22). In fact, "as opposed to duplicitous people, those with divided hearts, those who are simple have no other concern than to do the will of God, to observe his precepts; their whole existence is an expression of this disposition of heart, this rectitude."[2]

Simplicity as the total and unreserved self-giving to the Lord and His will expresses itself in the way we act and adorn ourselves. Functional jewelry must reveal that the center of our lives is in our commitment to Christ and not in a self-serving display of ostentatious ornaments. An undivided heart will show its full loyalty to our Savior in an unambiguous life style of service to him and to others. The principle of simplicity in the selection of functional jewelry, then, means that such jewelry must witness to the fact that we live an unpretentious and irreproachable life exclusively oriented toward our Savior and Lord. This is indeed singleness of heart-simplicity.[3]

"*Modesty*" is used by Paul in his discussion of proper Christian adornment (1 Tim 2:9), and by it he meant a self-respect determined by one's claim to be living a life pleasing to the Lord. Consequently it leads to the avoidance of excess or extremes and acknowledges and abides by the limits of propriety. What is proper is not simply what society has established but primarily what has been specified in the instructions given

---

[1]Consult, Otto Bauernfeind, "*Haplous, haplotes*," *Theological Dictionary of the NT*, vol. 1, pp. 386, 387; R. L. Scheef, "Simplicity," *Interpreter's Dictionary of the Bible*, vol. 4, pp. 360, 361, writes, "In the NT the primary word for 'simplicity' is *haplotes*, which characteristically designates an undivided loyalty, purity in devotion as to Christ; but the term can also mean 'wholeness of heart' in the sense of 'generosity' or 'liberality'" (p. 360); Burkhard Gartner, "Simplicity, Sincerity, Uprightness," *New International Dictionary of NT Theology*, vol. 3, pp. 371-72; and Tim Schramm, "*Haplotes* simplicity, sincerity, uprightness," *Exegetical Dictionary of the NT*, vol. 1, pp. 123-124.

[2]Spicq, "*Haplotes*," *Lexicon*, vol. 1, p. 170.

[3]Scriven, "Ring," p. 58, defines simplicity as "the attempt to master greed, to overcome extravagance, to live without the proud showiness that can only deepen the pain of the poor who cannot afford what we display. Simplicity is a focus on the inner person, not the outer person; it is concern for others, no preoccupation with one's self." Although there is much truth in it, its major weakness is that simplicity is defined in terms of what it rejects rather than in terms of what it is. Simplicity is fundamentally a positive wholeheartedly commitment to God, the outflow of which is a life that displays that commitment in the way we deal with our possessions, financial resources and personal adornment. Scriven seems, perhaps unintentionally, to introduce a dichotomy between the inner and the outer person when suggesting that simplicity is centered in the inner not the outer person. In biblical thinking simplicity is not just an inner experience but also one that is embodied in our exterior demeanor.

by the apostle to the community of believers. Where Christian instruction coincides with societal values, this benefits the Church in that the values of its members are not in conflict with those of non-believers. In short, modest functional jewelry avoids extremes of display and is loyal to the Christian parameters for personal propriety.

"*Economy*" is difficult to define because it varies from person to person. What is inexpensive may in the long run prove to be expensive and the expensive may show itself to be more economical. In the biblical texts dealing with jewelry the principle of economy is not emphasized. However, the Bible does have much to say about stewardship of our financial resources and our accountability to God.[1] In the case of functional jewelry "economy" probably means that since in general expensive jewelry tends to be ostentatious we must avoid buying it and that investing significant amounts of money in what is, from the biblical point of view, of little value for the Christian life violates our responsibility as stewards of God.

3. Symbol of Social Status

Jewelry as a symbol of social status and power is in a very few cases tolerated in the Bible but in other cases it is disapproved. This phenomenon must alert us to be very careful when dealing with this particular function of jewelry in the church. Here we face a situation in which cultural practices around the world may play a significant role in whatever is decided by the church. For instance, military officers usually display on their uniforms insignias and medals that serve to identify their acts of courage and their social role. This is a well-accepted cultural practice and the church could consider this type of jewelry as functional. Another example: The graduation ring appears to serve only to signal our superiority over others who, for a variety of reasons, could not accomplish what we have accomplished in the academic world. Is this a piece of proper functional jewelry? Hardly. But perhaps the governing principle is that any action, attitude, or symbol that would introduce unnecessary social distinctions among believers must be carefully evaluated and whenever possible laid at the foot of the cross, where there is equality in sin and grace. The emphasis should be placed in that which unites, not what separates.

---

[1]See, Angel Manuel Rodríguez, *Stewardship Roots: Toward a Theology of Stewardship, Tithe and Offerings* (Silver Spring, MD: Stewardship Department, 1994).

4. Principles versus Standards

The standard on jewelry (rejection of ornamental jewelry; restrictive use of functional jewelry) and the principles regulating the use of functional jewelry (e.g., modesty) have permanent relevance across time and culture. Those principles can and should be used to determine what is appropriate with respect to *functional jewelry*. In this particular case the church should not provide a list of what is or is not appropriate, but must give general guidance and allow church members, under the guidance of the Spirit, to apply to each specific cultural practice the biblical principles. We must acknowledge that there are areas in the Christian life where the individual and his or her Lord must decide what to do. This is in fact a sign of Christian and spiritual maturity. It is possible and even probable that some may misuse this freedom, but that argument should not be employed to deny the freedom granted to us by the Bible itself.

B. Dangers Associated with the Standard on Jewelry

Any Christian standard can be misused and misapplied, thereby losing its original positive intention and contribution to the well-being of the believer. The biblical standard on jewelry is certainly no exception. We will explore some of the dangers we may confront when emphasizing acceptance of the standard on jewelry and at the same time we will give some suggestions on how to deal with them in our own lives.

1. Sin and Jewelry

There is no doubt that in the Bible sin is much more than a particular action that damages the perpetrator or someone else. *Sin* is the condition under which we exist; it has corrupted our nature to the point that whatever we do needs to be mediated to God through Christ in order for Him to accept it. No action of ours, be it "good" or "bad," is untainted by *sin*. One could probably say that *sin* precedes sin as an evil act. This sinful state and environment in which we exist will not be eradicated until the glorious manifestation of our Savior and Lord, Jesus Christ, at his Second Coming.

Meanwhile, the Spirit works in our hearts, not allowing our sinful nature to rule over us to lead us into sinful behavior. The dominion of sin over us is strengthened and even actualized in our sinful acts. It is not a trivialization of sin to define it as acts committed against the will of God that are damaging to us and, in many cases, to those around us. Sin is killing someone, stealing, working on Sabbath, because in those sinful acts the dominion of sin over us is actualized. Overcoming those sinful acts is a victory over sin as an act and also as a state. This is the kind of victory that the Lord wants us to enjoy.

The fact that the standard of jewelry most directly deals with exterior acts does not trivialize sin[1] but on the contrary informs us how the Spirit can limit the power, dominion, and inroads of sin in our lives. One could say that obedience to God's specific commands is a proclamation of Christ's lordship in our lives. This obviously does not mean that our nature has been freed once and for all from its sinfulness; but it does mean that we are joyfully looking forward to the time when this will take place.

2. Legalism and Jewelry

The most threatening danger faced by those who emphasize obedience to the Law of God and to specific biblical standards is legalism. Legalism distorts obedience by creating a religious monstrosity that destroys the very essence of the Christian message of salvation exclusively in Christ, and in the process creates in the individual a sense of pride. This threat is faced not only by those who accept the biblical standard on jewelry but by anyone who seeks to obey the Lord. In the case of jewelry, a *legalistic* removal of ornamental jewelry and the use of simple, modest and economical functional jewelry destroys the very intent of the standard because instead of self-denial and humility it leads to selfishness and pride.

Legalism always is accompanied by a judgmental attitude. In our the wearing of jewelry those who accept the biblical standard on jewelry may be tempted to feel superior to those not fully committed to it. Obviously we could say the same thing about Sabbath observance, tithing, or doing missionary work. Hence, the issue is not jewelry but the deceptiveness of the human heart that some times takes what is good, obedience to God, and transforms it into a means of self-accomplishment and pride. What is needed is an awareness of the fact that genuine obedience is a humble expression of gratitude to our Savior and to God for what they have done for us on the cross. Our obedience is an offering of love to God and He does not expect us to compare what we bring to Him with what other human beings are offering Him. Whenever we try to assist others in their Christian experience it must be done in love and not in condemnation and rejection.

---

[1]This is an argument used by Dennis H. Braun, *A Seminar on Adventists, Adornment and Jewelry*, pp. 50-51, which he took from George R. Knight, *The Pharisee's Guide to Perfect Holiness* (Nampa, ID: Pacific Press, 1992), p. 51.

3. Principles, Jewelry, Houses, Cars?

There is no question that the principles of simplicity, modesty and economy extend beyond the sphere of personal adornment and dress. We must personally seek to apply them in the broadest possible way to every dimension of our walk with God. Perhaps at times the church has unintentionally tended to underline their applicability only to the area of dress and ornamentation. If that were the case, the call to the church is to broaden the application of those principles to many other aspects of the Christian experience. However, in this task the church needs to be extremely careful not to create new standards that could unnecessarily burden church members.

No one should expect the church to decide for its members what is a modest and economical car, a modest house, or a simple watch. Those are areas where the church should only teach the Christian principles and challenge its members to use them as they make personal decisions in their daily life. The obvious question is, Why could we not do the same when it comes to the standard of ornamental jewelry? The answer is simple: The Bible itself has set up for us this particular standard and therefore the church can and must teach it. In areas where the Scriptures speak clearly we have no choice but to listen to it. The application of the principles governing the standard on jewelry to other areas must be left to the work of the Spirit in the hearts of those who claim to live a life pleasing to the Lord.

4. Gender and Jewelry

There has also been a tendency in the church to address the issue of jewelry almost exclusively in reference to its female members. This is to some extent understandable, if we take into consideration that until recently most ornamental jewelry worn in the western world was mainly by women and that some of the biblical passages were directed specifically to them. But it is now clear that in biblical times the issue of jewelry affected both genders and that today jewelry is being used by both men and women. Therefore, we should not deal with this topic as if it were a female problem, but look at it for what it really is, a part of the human predicament.

C. Conclusion

The subject of jewelry should not be allowed to distract our attention from the good news of salvation through faith in Christ. It is within the context of the gospel that we should teach the biblical standard on jewelry;

otherwise we will fall into the trap of legalism or judgmentalism. In teaching the biblical standard on jewelry we must make clear that ornamental jewelry is rejected but that functional jewelry is not. Making a distinction between these two may prove at times to be somewhat difficult, but it not need to be that difficult.

Functional jewelry is easily identified in most cultures and therefore we must allow cultural practices to inform us. In other words, functional jewelry is not defined by personal wishes but by respected cultural beliefs and practices. For instance, the church must be willing to acknowledge that in some cultures a necklace is used to indicate that the woman wearing it is married; while in other cultures is it is simply an ornament. In the first situation the necklace is acceptable but in the other its is to be rejected. In the selection of functional jewelry the Christian must follow the biblical principles of modesty, simplicity and economy.

This approach to the question of jewelry is based on the fact that the Bible combines a specific standard on jewelry (rejection of ornamental jewelry and restrictive use of functional jewelry) with a set of principles to be used in the selection of functional jewelry. In order for the church to remain faithful to the Scriptural witness it needs to teach both elements.

REASONS FOR THE BIBLICAL STANDARD ON JEWELRY

X

We hardly find an explicit reason given by the biblical writers for the standard on jewelry. In fact, seldom do we find a biblical justification for a particular command from the Lord. As the covenant God, He informed His people what He expected of them in terms of how to relate to Him and to each other. It is mainly through theological analysis that we are able to uncover some of the reasons for what the Lord required from His people. In the case of jewelry a series of concepts associated with it provides some understanding of the usefulness of the standard.

A. Standard on Jewelry and God's Will

The fundamental reason given in the Bible for obedience to any of the commandments is that they are the expression of God's unquestionable will for His people. This authoritative approach is not popular in our age where authority is questioned and everything is evaluated not merely in terms of what is reasonable but particularly in terms of the benefit to be gained from it. If there is nothing for me in it there is no reason to bother with it. What is usually overlooked in this approach is that the expression of God's will for us always brings with it tremendous benefits to those who accept it. We may not want to argue that obedience to God's will should be based on selfish motives, but the fact is that God's will for us is always good.

God's call to unquestionable obedience has the fundamental purpose of assisting us to overcome self-centeredness. Submission to His will requires from us to acknowledge that He, as Creator and Redeemer, has the authority to define for us what is the best for our lives. Submission to His will is essentially an act of self-denial, which is precisely what He intends to achieve through the command. He is in fact attempting to re-create and restore us to our original condition of complete harmony with Him. Hence, when God informs us that it is not in accordance with His will for us to wear ornamental jewelry He is teaching us self-denial in the way we adorn ourselves. Very often the natural human reaction is to oppose or question God's will because fallen human nature is not interested in self-denial. We want to be ourselves; to be the way we are. But what the Lord is stating is that the way we are today is not the way He created us in the beginning and that He is interested in helping us become what we *really* should be.

Each one of God's commands is a call to self-denial, an invitation to put aside our will for our lives and accept His will for us. Replacing our will with His will is something done by the Spirit for our own benefit and not for God's benefit. He does not *need* our submission to Him; *we need* it because it is in this act that we become that for which we were created and what we would in fact like to be. God wants to heal us from the disease of self-centeredness and this is done, among many other ways, through the call to self-denial in the way we adorn ourselves.

B. Standard on Jewelry and Human Value

Society has conditioned us to believe that our personal value is dependent on such things as academic degrees, wealth, the type of car we drive, the house and place where we live, and the way we look. The biblical standard on jewelry is an indictment against a society that enslaves us by destroying our self-worth in order to attempt to build it up through the addition to our lives of external and superfluous things. It would appear that in order for world-wide economic systems to survive they must first diminish our self-image, then persuade us to believe that to be attractive, influential, and powerful we need to *buy* what they offer us. The Bible wants us to break away from such enslaving social and economic power.[1]

The Bible re-affirms our self-worth on the basis of creation and redemption. God created us in His image and did not associate that intrinsic value with external ornamental jewelry (Gen 3:21). Neither does Christ expect us to beautify ourselves in order to be of value to him. We are wealthy in him, but this is the wealth and value of a life lived in fellowship with him. If there is a time when the biblical standard on jewelry should be upheld it is now. Social oppression is always evil, but we tend to overlook some of its less obvious expressions. Consequently, we tend quietly to submit to it and in the process our self-dignity is diminished.

---

[1]Gary Krause, "Dying for an Image," *Adventist Review*, August 21, 1997, writes: "Granted, we all want to feel wanted, needed, valuable. But it's easy to fall for the media hype and start looking for self-worth in the wrong place. The images promise much but don't last. As Adventists we must fight against conformity to society's images . . . Our self-worth must come not from the beauty industries' changing ideals, but from our eternal identity: 'members of God's household' (Eph. 2:19, NIV), 'children of the kingdom' (Matt. 13:38, NRSV), 'jewels in a crown' (Zech. 9:16, NIV)" (p. 12). See also the excellent article by Leslie Kay, "This Jewelry Thing," *Adventist Review*, August 1998, p. 28.

Our jewelry standard is a rebellion against this pervasive social demand and a reaffirmation of our value in Christ.

C. Standard on Jewelry and a Restful Life

There is great unrest in the human heart which reveals itself in different ways, including the way humans adorn themselves. Rest is a fundamental human need. It is true that we realize ourselves through our actions, for we are dynamic agents and there is nothing wrong with this aspect of our existence. But because of sin, the function of our actions and deeds has been distorted and they have become the means through which we seek personal self-realization apart from Christ. It was probably in response to this problem that Jesus said: "Come to me, all you who are weary and burdened, and I will give you rest" (Matt 11:28).

Peter associates the standard on jewelry with "a gentle and quiet spirit," that is to say with reliance on God and peacefulness (1 Pet 3:4). The standard on jewelry is a call to a life of rest in Christ. Peter seems to be saying that the use of ornamental jewelry tends to reveal a restless spirit, an unfulfilled quest for inner peace and tranquility and he wants us to indicate through our personal adornment that we have found rest in Christ. It is not necessary for those who follow Jesus to sew "fig leaves together and [make] coverings for themselves" (Gen 3:7).

D. Standard on Jewelry and Humility

In the Bible jewelry is at times associated with pride, ostentatiousness, and idolatry (e.g. Isa 3:18-21; Gen 35:2-4). It is considered to be an expression of our power and the way we see ourselves and others. Pride is fundamentally an idolatrous self-perception that makes us believe we are more than we really are. This self-deception has an impact on the way we treat others since we perceive them as inferiors to us. External adornment tends to express and feed this pride and as such it can displace our love for God. By calling us to set aside ornamental jewelry the Lord invites us to a humble walk with him that will contribute to deepening our love for Him, to the breaking down of social barriers and to teach us to rely on his divine power in our lives (1 Pet 3:4).

The Lord is trying to achieve that same goal in many other ways, but the standard on jewelry contributes to it. Therefore it is counterproductive for a Christian to be proud of not wearing ornamental jewelry because the standard itself is a call to Christian humility. Humility should not be understood to mean that no attention is to be given to our external appearance. Remember, the Bible does not condemn all forms of external adornment but qualifies it as simple, modest and economical.

E. Standard on Jewelry, God's Grace and the Community of Believers

The Scriptures put significant emphasis on remembering what the Lord has done for us in the past because that remembrance has an impact on both the present and the future. Humans forget, but God does not want us to forget His loving kindness toward us. It is interesting to note that the rejection of jewelry is associated with a humble re-commitment to Him that relies on His forgiving grace (e.g. Exod 33:5,6). Then, it could be suggested that the implementation of the standard on jewelry in the life of believers can function as a reminder of the fact that God, out of His loving grace, did not require from them to improve themselves in order to be accepted by Him. Gold and silver did not buy our redemption, but the blood of the Son of God (1 Pet 1:18,19).

This transfer from darkness to the light of Christ incorporated us into the family of God. Peter speaks of holiness in the context of jewelry in the sense of being part of the people of God, that is to say belonging to Him and to the community of believers (1 Pet 3:5). The Christian standard on jewelry sets boundaries and contributes to the external identity of the members of that community. This requires a renewal and re-commitment to our communal understanding of a biblical and Christian life style and implies a rejection of a private conception of it.[1]

F. Standard on Jewelry and Re-creation

The Scripture states that a life adorned by the grace of God, and not with ornamental jewelry, is pleasing to God (1 Pet 3:4). God's value system governs the life of His people. Sin has distorted our understanding of true

---

[1]In this area the comments of Monte Sahlin are worth quoting: "One of the ways in which a fellowship of believers can support and encourage one another in their spiritual journey is by agreeing on certain minimum disciplines that will undergird their individual walks with Christ. Church standards are minimums spiritual disciplines that all members of a particular Christian fellowship agree to be the starting point for their spiritual growth. Those in that fellowship covenant that they will support one another and hold one another accountable for at least these minimum standards of spiritual discipline. We should not regard believers who choose not to enter into the covenant as evil or deficient in commitment and fervor. But in making that choice, those believers have also chosen to live outside that particular fellowship, because the covenant of accountability and encouragement is integral to the fabric of the fellowship" ("Church Standards Today: Where are We Going?," *Ministry*, October, 1989, pp. 14, 15. That type of agreement on basic biblical standards existed among Adventist and needs to be re-affirmed.

values, but God is described as willing to assist us in recognizing them. When we follow the biblical instruction on personal adornment we develop, through the power of the Spirit, new values, even new aesthetic taste. In fact we are incorporating into our lives God's values and aesthetics. Obviously, this is not the only way God is doing that, but it is one of the them.

God is willing to use the biblical standard on jewelry to transform us into His likeness. By putting it into practice we are imitating God, becoming more like Him, and accepting the principles of personal aesthetics that are held by Him in real value.

G. Standard on Jewelry and the Lordship of Christ

The good news of the gospel is that Christ died in our place bearing our sin and guilt in order for us to be justified by faith in him. We can claim him as our Savior. But the gospel also invites us to claim him as Lord of our lives. It is important to remember that his lordship is not restricted to a spiritual or religious experience detached from the reality of our daily life. He is to be Lord over every aspect of life.

Adventists have insisted that Christ is Lord of our time, space, intellect, wealth, and bodies. In fact, we have gone so far as to say that he is Lord even over what we eat, informing us the type of food we should consume. No secular dimension exists in the life of a Christian. The standard on jewelry informs us that he is also Lord over the way we adorn ourselves. Our values express themselves by the way we adorn our bodies, telling others that which is of primary importance in our lives. We cannot be permanently true to ourselves if what we do and the way we look are not in agreement with our inner values and convictions.

When we look at ourselves in the mirror, the absence of ornamental jewelry should remind us that Christ is indeed Lord of our lives. But at the same time it should remind us that he wants us to demonstrate his lordship in our daily life by incorporating the principles of simplicity, modesty and economy in all that we do.

H. Conclusion

The Adventist standard on jewelry is supported by contextual analysis of the biblical texts, the Christian use of those passages to develop a standard on jewelry, and by fundamental religious, theological, and pragmatic reasons. Too much is at stake for the church to relax or reject the expression of God's will for His people in this area. What is needed is a clear understanding on the part of pastors, teachers, and church leaders of this standard to make it relevant to our church members around the world.

A particular responsibility rests on the shoulders of those working in the church with our young people as they pass on to the new generation a standard that goes against the grain of society. Perhaps this is the kind of challenge our young people need: a call to indict society in an area that affects their self-image in a very direct way. In this task the entire church should provide moral support by living the biblical standard on jewelry.

Appendix I

1972 Autumn Council
of the
GENERAL CONFERENCE COMMITTEE

General Actions

October 14-29, 1972
Mexico City, Mexico

DISPLAY AND ADORNMENT

The basic philosophy of Christian standards as understood by Seventh-day Adventists is set forth on page 221 to *The Church Manual* (1971 edition):

"Standing amid the perils of the last days, facing a judgment that will culminate in the establishment of universal righteousness, and bearing the responsibility of speedily carrying the last offer of salvation to the world, let us with true heart consecrate ourselves to God, body, soul, and spirit, determining to maintain the high standards of living that must characterize those who wait for the return of their Lord."

In the light of the above declaration the one who has a personal and loving relationship with the self-sacrificing Christ, will abstain from the wearing of jewelry and all adornments that give evidence of pride and are not in keeping with the Christian principles of humility, self-denial and sacrifice. Christ will adorn his heart and life with Christian virtues, and he will gladly heed the counsel set forth in 1 Timothy 2:9, 10, which, while addressed specifically to women, contains principles applicable to all Christians:

"Women again must dress in becoming manner, modestly and soberly, not with elaborate hair styles, not decked out with gold or pearls, or expensive clothes, but with good deeds, as befits women who claim to be religious." (NEB)

Peter enunciates similar ideals in 1 Peter 3:3, 4, "Your beauty should reside, not in outward adornment—the braiding of the hair, or jewelry, or dress—but in the inmost center of your being, with its imperishable ornament, a gentle, quiet spirit, which is of high value in the sight of God." (NEB)

These principles are summarized in *Testimonies*, Vol. 3, page 366:

"To dress plainly, abstaining from display of jewelry and ornaments of every kind, is in keeping with our faith."

The following statement adapted by the General Conference Spring Meeting (April 1, 1971) further amplifies the basic philosophy of the Seventh-day Adventist Church on Christian standards.

"According to divine plan the remnant church is to separate itself from the world in its unique role of preparing a people to meet their Lord. As the great controversy between Christ and Satan comes to its climax, the forces of evil will attack the church and its standards.

"If the church follows the low standard of the world in such matters as dress, music, reading, eating, drinking, or recreation, it will become separated from the channel of divine power. 'Christ's followers are to seek to improve the moral tone of the world, under the influence of the impartation of the Spirit of God. They are not to come down to the world's level, thinking that by doing this they will uplift it. In words, in dress, in spirit, in everything, there is to be a marked distinction between Christians and worldlings. This distinction has a convincing influence upon worldlings. They see that the sons and daughters of the Lord do separate themselves from the world, and that the Lord binds them up with Himself. . . Who is willing to be raised to the highest level?'—E. G. White, *That I May Know Him*, p. 305

"Seventh-day Adventist Christians are therefore under obligation to study carefully their conduct, personal appearance, and attitudes in order to attain to this highest level of living. In these days of extremes in conformity and nonconformity each individual may find in the guidebooks–the Bible and the writings of Ellen G. White—a clear understanding of life patterns that will properly reflect the Saviour.

"While we acknowledge that the quality of an individual's Christianity cannot be gauged solely by external criteria, we do know that his outward appearance will reveal either conformity to the world or to the Word. 'The external appearance is an index to the heart.'—*Ibid*, p. 312. The Seventh-day Adventist Christian will strive to reach the standard set by the Word. He will recognize that true conformity to that Word will be revealed by a progressive transformation of life based on a deepening and lasting relationship with Christ. In sharing the life of Christ he comes to accept a different life style which involves his whole person. He will give evidence of this by his conduct, personal appearance, and his attitudes. 'Adapt yourselves no longer to the pattern of this present world, but let your minds be remade and your whole nature thus transformed. Then you will be able to discern the will of God, and to know what is good, acceptable, and perfect.' (Romans 12:2, NEB).

"Because the family is a God-appointed unit, we believe that a Christian life style is best born and nurtured in the family setting where children learn early that true love encourages willing obedience and self-control. Physical growth is then accompanied by commitment to the Christian way of life, development of character, and acceptance of Biblical ideals."

On the basis of such counsel with regard to Christian display and adornment,

Voted

1. That the principles of self-denial, economy, and simplicity should be applied to all areas of life—to our persons, our homes, our churches, and our institutions.

2. That in the area of personal adornment necklaces, earrings, bracelets, jewelled and other ornamental rings* should not be worn. Articles such as ornamental watches, broaches, cufflinks, etc., should be chosen in harmony with the Christian principles of simplicity, modesty and economy.

3. That our pastors, evangelists, and Bible instructors present fully to the candidates for baptism the Bible principles regarding display and adornment; point out the dangers of clinging to customs and practices that may be inimical to spiritual development; press the claims of the gospel upon the conscience of the candidates, encouraging careful self-examination concerning the motives involved in decisions that must be made; and acquaint the candidate with the inspired counsel given by Ellen G. White.

As Seventh-day Adventists we believe in the priesthood of all believers. Each soul has direct access to God through Christ, and is accountable to Him for his life and witness. The spiritual condition of the church is basically the sum of the spiritual experience of each individual. In view of this, we urge all our members to commit themselves wholeheartedly to the principles set forth above.

Beyond this, and because of the special opportunities that rest with leadership to help the church reach its full potential of spiritual power, we expect our church officers, ministers and their wives, teachers, and other Seventh-day Adventist workers to strongly support these principles through their public testimony and example.

In this final hour of earth's history, the church must not lower its standards, blur its identity, or muffle its witness, but must with renewed emphasis give strong support to the standards and principles that have distinguished the remnant church throughout its history and have kept it separate from the world.

* "In some countries the custom of wearing the marriage ring is considered imperative, having become in the minds of the people, a criterion of virtue, and hence is not regarded as an ornament. Under such circumstances we have no disposition to condemn the practice." –*Church Manual*, 1971 edition, p. 212.

Appendix II

Jewelry—a Clarification and Appeal:
An Action Voted at the North American Division 1986 Year-end Meeting

At the 1972 Annual Council the General Conference officers gave counsel regarding the wedding band in North America. An examination of this statement reveals the following salient points:

1. Ministers were counseled not to perform ring ceremonies, since the wearing of the wedding band still "is not regarded as obligatory" or an "imperative" custom in North America.

2. Pastors, evangelists, and Bible instructors were urged to present to candidates for baptism the Bible principle regarding display and ornaments, encouraging careful self-examination concerning the motives involved in deciding whether to wear the wedding band.

3. Baptism was not to be denied to converts who conscientiously felt they should wear the wedding band.

4. Church officers, ministers and their wives, teachers, and other SDA workers were urged to give strong support to the standards and principles that have distinguished the remnant church.

The Annual Council of the same year also stated very clearly its position on personal adornment as follows:

"That in the area of personal adornment necklaces, earrings, bracelets, rings (including engagement rings) should not be worn. Articles such as watches, broaches, cuff links, tie clasps, etc., should be chosen in harmony with the Christian principles of simplicity, modesty, and economy."

It seems, therefore, that in 1972 the church had a strong desire to maintain a high standard in the matter of personal adornment. Yet it also recognized the simple wedding band as being in a category distinct from that of jewelry work for ornamental purposes.

The *Church Manual* likewise states the principles involved in the matter of personal adornment (see pp. 145, 146: "Dress"). Included in this particular section is the following statement:

"In some countries the custom of wearing the marriage ring is considered imperative, having become, in the minds of the people, a criterion of virtue, and hence it is not regarded as an ornament. Under such circumstances we have no disposition to condemn the practice" (*Church Manual*, 146).

During the intervening years large numbers of members who have come from areas in the world where wearing a wedding band is an accepted and necessary symbol of marriage have joined the church in North America. A growing number of employees from such areas have also come to serve the church at all levels. In North America are many loyal, clear-thinking members who believe that conditions have changed greatly since the 1890s when Ellen White's counsel was given and that her statement "in countries where the custom is imperative, we have no burden to condemn those who have their marriage ring; let them wear it if they can do so conscientiously" is now applicable in North America.

Across the division the position concerning the wedding band has not been uniform, and possibly it never will be. However, there has developed an ambivalence on the part of many, and the lack of consistency has caused embarrassment and even hardship and misunderstanding. It has also obscured the church's position on the wearing of jewelry.

In light of these and other factors, it is

Voted,

1. To reaffirm the principles regarding personal adornment as outlined in the *Church Manual*, the 1972 Annual Council action, and the General Conference officers' statement of October 2, 1972.

2. To affirm that the wearing of jewelry is unacceptable and is a denial of the principles enunciated in the Bible and Spirit of Prophecy concerning personal adornment.

3. To recognize that, in harmony with the position stated in the *Church Manual* (pp. 145, 146), some church members in the North American Division as in other parts of the world feel that wearing a simple marriage band is a symbol of faithfulness to the marriage vow and to declare that such persons should be fully accepted in the fellowship and service of the church.

4. To make an immediate appeal to our people for a commitment to simplicity in lifestyle and by pen, voice, and example to halt the rising tide of worldly attitudes and practices that have made their subtle appearance within the church in recent years.

Appendix III

Statement from E. G. White on Jewelry and Personal Ornamentation[1]

1. Biblical Foundation

Have not our sisters sufficient zeal and moral courage to place themselves without excuse upon the Bible platform? The apostle has given most explicit directions on this point: I will therefore . . . that women adorn themselves in modest apparel, with shamefacedness and sobriety; not with braided hair, or gold, or pearls, or costly array; but (which becometh women professing godliness) with good works." Here the Lord, through His apostle, speaks expressly against the wearing of gold. Let those who have had experience see to it that they do not lead others astray on this point by their example. That ring encircling your finger may be very plain, but it is useless, and the wearing of it has a wrong influence upon others. (4 *T* 360)

2. Biblical Principles of Simplicity and Modesty

We have not time now to give anxious thought as to what we shall eat and drink, and wherewithal we shall be clothed. Let us live simply, and work in simplicity. Let us dress in such a modest, becoming way that we will be received wherever we go. Jewelry and expensive dress will not give us influence, but the ornament of a meek and quiet spirit–the result of

---

[1]Some have commented, based on photographs of E. G. White, that sometimes she wore jewelry (Wheeler, "Adventist Standards," p. 10; and Land, "Plain Dress," p. 47). Concerning this question, Norma Collins, from the White Estate, Washington, DC, writes: "Ellen White never had a string of pearls, and there is no picture of her wearing a kind of necklace. She sometimes wore a broach to hold her detachable collar in place, and she had one pin that she specially liked, a gift from Sister Kerr in Hawaii, which she deemed 'serviceable and not showy at all.' Ella White, her granddaughter, had a string of very small shells that she sometimes wore around her neck, You can see it very plainly in the family picture on page 221 of volume 5 of the E. G. White Biography, *The Early Elmshaven Years*. It is my personal opinion that this string of shells was given to Ella by perhaps a native of one of the islands of the South Pacific as the family returned from Australia in 1900. Or maybe she got it somewhere else during their stay in Australia" (November 19,1991, Q&A 10-E-3). Concerning the shell necklace Tim Poirier, also from the E. G. White Estate in Washington, DC, wrote: "According to the White family, on Ellen White's return trip from Australia they stopped at a Pacific island where Ellen White was presented a shell necklace in commemoration of her visit. This is what her granddaughter, Ella, is wearing in the picture. Many years ago, (I have been unable to find our when), a picture of the White family was printed in the *Review*, and at that time the best judgment was that the proper thing to do was to have the shell necklace airbrushed out. We would differ with that judgment today, but, at any rate, this picture was filed among the other photographs. When the 6-volume *EGW Biography* was published the same picture appeared in volume 6 (p. 243), quite innocently, I believe, since volume 5 of the same series (already published) has another picture of the White family where a shell necklace is plainly shown around Ella's neck (p. 221). In fact, this picture showing Ella's necklace has been in print since 1960 in *The Spirit of Prophecy Treasury Chest*, p. 102, (the Voice of Prophecy textbook for the prophetic guidance course.)"-Tim Poirier in e-mail communication to Brian Holland, August 16, 1994.

devotion to the service of Christ–will give us power with God. Kindness and forethought for those about us are qualities precious in the sight of heaven. If you have not given attention to the acquirement of these graces, do so now, for you have no time to lose (9 *MR* 120).

It is evident that fashionable ladies are losing the consciousness that true beauty of dress consists in its simplicity, rather than in ruffles, flounces, puffs, tucks, and elaborate embroidery. The arranging of jewelry, sashes, laces, and unnecessary ornaments upon their persons, alone must occupy a large share of their time. It is apparent that women professing godliness have their minds and thoughts absorbed with, "What shall we eat? or, What shall we drink? or, Wherewithal shall we be clothed?" It really seems to be the mission and object of a large class of women to exhibit their wardrobe. Their burdens, trials, and perplexities, are mostly in regard to dress. (*Health Reformer*, March 1, 1874, pr. 1)

3. Jewelry and Personal Value

Christians are not to decorate the person with costly array of expensive ornaments. All this display imparts no value to the character. The Lord desires every converted person to put away the idea that dressing as worldlings dress will give value to our influence. The ornamentation of the person with jewels and luxurious things is a species of idolatry. This needless display reveals a love for those things which are supposed to place a value upon the person. It gives evidence to the world of a heart destitute of the inward adornment. Expensive dress and adornments of jewelry give an incorrect representation of the truth that should always be represented as of the highest value. An overdressed, outwardly adorned person bears the sign of inward poverty. A lack of spirituality is revealed. (6 *MR* 159)

Sinners are under a fearful deception. They despise and reject the Saviour. They do not realize the value of the pearl offered to them, and cast it away, rendering to their Redeemer only insult and mockery. Many a woman decks herself with rings and bracelets, thinking to gain admiration, but she refuses to accept the pearl of great price, which would secure for her sanctification, honor, and eternal riches. What an infatuation is upon the minds of many! They are more charmed with earthly baubles, which glitter and shine, than with the crown of immortal life, God's reward for loyalty. "Can a maid forget her ornaments, or a bride her attire? yet my people have forgotten me days without number" (Jer. 2:32). (1 *SM* 400).

4. Jewelry and Self-Denial

Those who have bracelets, and wear gold and ornaments, had better take these idols from their persons and sell them, even if it should be for much less than they gave for them, and thus practice self-denial. Time is too short to adorn the body with gold or silver or costly apparel. I know a good work can be done in this line. Jesus, the Commander in the heavenly courts, laid aside His crown of royalty and His royal robe and stepped down from His royal throne, and clothed His divinity with the habiliments of humanity, and for our sakes became poor, that we through His poverty might come into possession of eternal riches, and yet the very ones for whom Christ has done everything that was possible to do to save the perishing souls from eternal ruin feel so little disposition to deny themselves anything they have money to buy. (9 *MR* 117).

God has made provision that ignorance need not exist. Those who have means are to take up their God-given responsibility. The poor are the purchase of the blood of the Son of God, and with God there is no respect of persons. The Lord says, "Sell that ye have, and give alms." Instead of hanging a necklace of gold and jewels about your neck, instead of adorning and decorating your mortal bodies, you are to deny yourself, take up your cross daily, and follow Jesus. You are to impart to others, and care for the destitute and the ignorant. (*Review & Herald*, March 17, 1896, pr. 8)

5. Jewelry, Idolatry and Humility

Jewelry which cost many hundreds of dollars has been given to Elder Simpson to be sold for the cause. There is no spirit of excitement in this movement. No fanaticism attends it. The truth takes hold of hearts; and men and women give their rings and bracelets although no call has been made for them to strip themselves of these idols. The work is earnest and quiet. The people take off their jewelry of their own freewill, and bring it to Elder Simpson as an offering up of their idols. (14 *MR* 250-51)

As Jacob thus reviewed the goodness and mercy of God to him, his own heart was subdued and humbled; and he had taken the most effectual way to reach the hearts of his children, and lead them to reverence the God of Heaven when they arrived at Bethel. Not in the least did any of his family hesitate to obey his commands. All that were with him delivered up their idols, and also their earrings, and he buried them under an oak near Shechem. The patriarch felt that humiliation before God was more in keeping with their position than was the wearing of gold and silver ornaments. (*Signs of the Times*, December 4, 1879, pr. 7).

6. Jewelry and Stewardship

Care for the Needy: There are many whose hearts have been so hardened by prosperity that they forget God, and forget the wants of their fellow man. Professed Christians adorn themselves with jewelry, laces, costly apparel, while the Lord's poor suffer for the necessaries of life. Men and women who claim redemption through a Saviour's blood will squander the means intrusted to them for the saving of other souls, and then grudgingly dole out their offerings for religion, giving liberally only when it will bring honor to themselves. These are idolaters (*Signs of the Times,* January 26, 1882).

Soul Winning: Shall those who profess the name of Christ see no attraction in the world's Redeemer? Will they be indifferent to the possession of truth and righteousness, and turn from the heavenly treasure to the earthly? Can you, my sister, use the Lord's money to purchase diamonds or any other jewels for any person? These cannot save one soul. They will not lead anyone to accept the saving truths for this time. Let us do nothing to encourage a vanity that is sinful. No, my sister, save the money you may be tempted to spend in this way, and place it where it will bring honor and glory to Christ. When your brother becomes anxious to secure the Pearl of great price, which is truth, pure, unadulterated truth, he will see that that which he now deems wisdom is vanity. (9 *MR* 119).

There is altogether too much self-indulgence, too much investing of money in houses, in adornments, in buying unnecessary things for display; and souls are perishing out of Christ. Men, women, and youth, according to their capacity, should be engaged in some part of the Lord's vineyard. Now is our time and opportunity; we are now in the midst of our God-given probation, in which we are to develop character after Christ's order. (*Review & Herald,* January 8, 1895, pr. 3).

7. Acceptance of the Standard

Preceded by Love to Christ and Conversion: There is no need to make the dress question the main point of your religion. There is something richer to speak of. Talk of Christ, and when the heart is converted everything that is out of harmony with the Word of God will drop off. . . . In order to teach men and women the worthlessness of earthly things, you must lead them to the living Fountain, and get them to drink of Christ, until their hearts are filled with the love of God, and Christ is in them, a well of water springing up onto everlasting life. (Ev 272).

Preceded by Commitment to Christ: If we are Christians, we shall follow Christ, even though the path in which we are to walk cuts right across our natural inclinations. There is no use in telling you that you must not wear this or that, for if the love of these vain things is in your heart, your laying off your adornments will only be like cutting the foliage off a tree. The inclinations of the natural heart would again assert themselves. (*CG*, 429-30).

Preceded by Love for the Truth: Today I have had an interview with one who is just taking her stand for the truth, but she is much adorned with gold bracelets and rings. I think she is good material, and will bear to hear kindly advice. The word must be presented: "Whose adorning let it not be that outward adorning of plaiting the hair, and of wearing of gold, or of putting on of apparel. But let it be the hidden man of the heart, in that which is not corruptible, even the ornament of a meek and quiet spirit, which is in the sight of God of great price" (1 Peter 3:3,4). I believe that this sister has received the truth and will practice the truth. If she loves the truth she will obey the words of Christ. (9 *MR* 118).

8. Functional Jewelry

Sign of Royalty: Mark how tender and pitiful the Lord is in His dealings with His creatures. He loves His erring child, and entreats him to return. The Father's arm is placed about His repentant son; the Father's garments cover his rags; the ring is placed upon his finger as a token of his royalty. And yet how many there are who look upon the prodigal not only with indifference, but with contempt. (*GW* 15).

Insignia of High Office: The appointment was decided upon, and to Joseph the astonishing announcement was made, "Forasmuch as God hath showed thee all this, there is none so discreet and wise as thou art: thou shalt be over my house, and according unto thy word shall all my people be ruled: only in the throne will I be greater than thou." The king proceeded to invest Joseph with the insignia of his high office. "And Pharaoh took off his ring from his hand, and put it upon Joseph's hand, and arrayed him in vestures of fine linen, and put a gold chain about his neck; and he made him to ride in the second chariot which he had; and they cried before him, Bow the knee." (*PP* 221).

Sign of Marriage: In countries where the custom is imperative, we have no burden to condemn those who have their marriage ring; let them wear it if they can do so conscientiously. . . (*TM* 181).

SELECTED BIBLIOGRAPHY

Archi, Alfonso. "Circulation d'objets en métal précieux de poids standardisé à Ebla." *Miscellanea Babylonica: Mélanges offerts a Maurice Bivot.* Rénnis par J-M Durand et J-R Kupper. Paris: Editions Recherche sur les Civilisations, 1985. Pp 25-33.

Bacchiocchi, Samuele. *Christian Dress and Adornment.* Berrien Springs, MI: Biblical Perspectives, 1995.

Balch, David L. *Let Wives be Submissive: The Domestic Code in 1 Peter.* Chico, CA: Scholars Press, 1981. Pp 80-113.

Bietz, R. R. "Jewelry - Yesterday and Today." *Review & Herald,* April 21, 1966. Pp 2-3, 9-10.

Budge, E. A. Wallis. *Amulets and Superstitions.* London: Oxford University Press, 1930.

Case, Steve, ed. *Valuegenesis: Shall We Dance -Rediscovering Christ Ordered Standards.* Riverside, CA: La Sierra University Press, 1996.

Churchman, Roland. "The Wedding Ring." *Spectrum* 6.1-2 (1974): 74-76.

Crews, Joe. *Colorful Cosmetics and Jewelry.* Roseville, CA: Amazing Facts, 1970.

Delafield, D. A. "Ornaments & Jewelry." *Review & Herald*, Nov. 30, 1972. Pp 6-7.

Doran, Sandra. "Dialogues: Judged Values." *Adventist Review*, April 18, 1996. P 15.

Dossin, Georges & Finet, André. *Correspondance feminine.* Archives Royales de Mari, Vol.X. Paris: Librairie Orientaliste Paul Geuthner, 1978.

Dudley, Roger L. with Gillespie, V. Bailey. *Faith in the Balance.* Riverside, CA: La Sierra University Press, 1992.

Fekkes III, Jan. "'His Bride has Prepared Herself': Rev 12-21 and Isaiah Nuptial Imagery." *Journal of Biblical Literature* 109 (1990):269-87.

Forbes, R. J. *Studies in Ancient Technology.* Leiden: E J Brill, 1965.

Francis, R. E. and Vandeman, George E. *God Believes in Jewelry*. Nampa, ID: Pacific Press, 1984.

Gorelick, Leonard and Gwinnett, John A. "The Ancient Near Eastern Cylinder Seal as Social Emblem and Status Symbol." *Journal of Near Eastern Studies* 49 (1990):45-56.

Greengus, Samuel. "Bridewealth in Sumerian Sources." *Hebrew Union College Annual* 61 (1990):25-88.

Grosz, Katarzyna. "Dowry and Brideprice in Nuzi." *Studies on the Civilization and Culture of Nuzi and Hurrians in Honor of Ernest R Lacheman*. Edited by M. A. Morrison and D. I. Owen. Winona Lake, IN: Eisenbrauns, 1981. Pp 161-82.

Harris, J. S. "An Introduction to the Study of Personal Ornaments of Precious, Semi-precious and Imitation Stones Used Throughout Biblical History." *Annual of Leeds University Oriental Society* 4 (1962-1963):49-83.

_____. "The Stones of the High Priest's Breastplate." *Annual of Leeds University Oriental Society* 5 (1963-1965):40-62.

Haulotte, Edgar. *Symbolique du vêtement selon la Bible*. Paris: Aubier, 1966.

Jones-Haldeman, Madelyn. "Adorning the Temple of God." *Spectrum* 20 (1989):49-59.

Korpel, Marjo Christina Annette. *A Rift in the Clouds: Ugaritic and Hebrew Descriptions of the Divine*. Münster: Ugarit-Verlag, 1990.

Kruger, Paul A. "The Symbolic Significance of the Hem (*kā nā f*) in 1 Samuel 15.27." *Text and Context: OT and Semitic Studies for F C Fensham*. Edited by W Claasen. Sheffield: JSOT Press, 1988. Pp 105-116.

Land, Gary. "Adventists in Plain Dress." *Spectrum* 20 (1989):42-48.

Maxwell-Hyslop, K. R. *Western Asiatic Jewellery*. London: Methuen, 1971.

Milgrom, Jacob. "Of Hems and Tassels." *Biblical Archaeology Review* 9 (1983):61-65.

Oppenheim, A. Leo. "The Golden Garments of the Gods." *Journal of Near Eastern Studies* 8 (1949):172-93.

Platt, Elizabeth E. "Jewelry of Bible Times and the Catalog of Isaiah 3:18-23." *Andrews University Seminary Studies* 17 (1979):71-84; 189-202.

Ray, Leslie. "On the Home Front:This Jewelry Thing." *Adventist Review*, August 1998. P 28.

Reader, William. "The Twelve Jewels of Revelation 21:19-20." *Journal of Biblical Literature* 100 (1981):433-57.

Rosenthal, Renate. *Jewellery in Ancient Times*. London: Cassell, 1973.

Roth, Martha T. *Babylonian Marriage Agreements 7th-3rd Centuries BC*. AOAT 222. Neukirchen-Vluyn: Neukirchener Verlag, 1984.

Sahlin, Monte. "Church Standards Today: Where are We Going?"*Ministry*, October 1989. Pp 13-17.

Scriven, Charles. "'I Didn't Recognize You With Your Ring.'" *Spectrum* 20.2 (1989): 56-59.

Spicq, Ceslas. *Saint Paul: Les Épitres Pastorales*. Paris: Gabalda, 1947. Pp 52-74.

Thompson, Cynthia L. "Hairstyles, Head-coverings, and St Paul: Portraits from Roman Corinth." *Biblical Archaeologist* 51 (June 1988):99-115.

_____."Rings of Gold-Neither 'Modest' nor 'Sensible.'" *Bible Review* 9 (Feb 1993):28-33,55.

Tuland, C. G. "Let's Stop Arguing Over the Wedding Ring." *Spectrum* 8.2 (1977):59-61.

Van Buren, E. D. "Amulets, Symbols or Idols?" *Iraq* 12 (1950):193-96.

Verner, David C. *The Household of God: The Social World of the Pastoral Epistles*. Chico, CA: Scholars Press, 1983. Pp 168-71.

Wallace, Howard N. *The Eden Narrative*. Atlanta, GA: Scholars Press, 1985. Pp65-99.